THE SMALL BUSINESS START-UP GUIDE

SECOND EDITION

Other books by Robert Sullivan:

United States Government - New Customer!
ISBN 1-882480-20-1

THE SMALL BUSINESS START-UP GUIDE

by Robert Sullivan

SECOND EDITION

INFORMATION INTERNATIONAL
Great Falls, Virginia

THE SMALL BUSINESS START-UP GUIDE
(SECOND EDITION)

Publisher: Information International
Copyright 1998, Robert A. Sullivan

DISCLAIMER

Library of Congress Cataloging-in-Publication Data

658.02   Sullivan, Robert Allen, 1940 Oct. 9-
SUL   The small business start-up guide : practical advice on starting and operating a small business / Robert Sullivan - 2nd ed. Great Falls, Va. Information International, ©1998

        340 p.; 21.6cm.
        Includes index

        Summary: A guide designed to increase the probability of success and avoid common trouble areas in starting and operating a small business. Gives practical advice on such topics as selecting the right business, partners, marketing, insurance, computers, writing and speaking effectively, and others.

        ISBN 1-882480-05-8
        LCCN 97-93259
1. Small business - Planning 2. Small Business - Management 3. New business enterprises - Planning 4. New business enterprises - Management I. Title

        658.02'2_dc21

Cartoons by Dave Carpenter

Printed in the United States of America

TABLE OF CONTENTS

Dedication...

In memory of Cedric Dettloff
...who taught me the value of education

And to
Mom and Dad

CREDITS

Writing a book is hard work. In fact, I doubt very many books are really written by a single individual. Although my name appears as the author, there really should be quite a list. I cannot possibly list all those who assisted and provided comments, but I take solace in the fact that they know who they are.

My special thanks to Bob Krell who reviewed the manuscript and provided numerous comments that improved the text and its messages. Bob also suggested highlighting the key messages throughout the text which we have called "truisms."

Special mention also goes to Tina Bailey, my CPA, who truly epitomizes that profession; and, most importantly, to Trish Phillips, without whose constant encouragement this book would not have made it to publication.

Robert A. Sullivan, May 1996

SECOND EDITION NOTES

I thought that revising *The Small Business Start-Up Guide* would be easy. Fix a spelling error, update a telephone number, correct some grammar mistakes and off to the printer. Was I wrong. First of all, reading something you wrote a year or two previously always seems awkward when revisited. As a result, there are changes on nearly every page. Furthermore, the Internet has made a major impact on small business and now commands its own entire chapter.

I hope you find this second edition useful. We have updated a lot of material and added new chapters and appendices. Major changes to this edition include the following:

- New small business glossary

- New Internet chapter greatly expanded information including using the Internet for marketing

- New Chapter, "Financing Your Business."

- New extensive appendix which contains small business contact information for all 50 states

- Information about doing business with the U.S. Government

Remember, starting a business is an adventure and potentially very rewarding. Get going now!

Robert Sullivan, September 1997

Whatsoever is rightly done,
however humble, is noble

... Henry Royce

PREFACE

Why is this book different? Good question! The title tells part of the story .... This book is a guide and not a text book. It provides practical explanations of important areas that you should consider when starting a new business. The type of business we're talking about is the small startup in which no significant formal capital investment is contemplated (at least not initially).

This book is written for those of you with a business idea but with only a vague idea of how to proceed. The information this book provides is meant to keep you out of trouble and help you avoid future problems. It is a guide for increasing your probability of success.

A visit to your local library or bookstore will turn up an incredible array of "business books." For the most part these books contain useful information on a number of topics and, as you might expect, some do it better than others. In my research I found that what is available falls into three general categories:

1. Get rich quick (with little or no effort)
2. Advice on very specific business topics
3. Compendiums of information

Although useful for the purpose for which they were written, no single text seemed to be a PRACTICAL guide for the first-time prospective business owner. The information is all there, it's just hard to find!

Get rich quick books are fun to read but provide very little useful information for most of us. Most detail the success story of a single individual who got very rich or very lucky or was in the right place at the right time. For most of us, however, success will require getting smart, planning, learning from others, and working hard. It will take some time, but this guidebook will help.

Books on various specific business topics, such as writing a business plan, raising capital, taxes, hiring and firing employees are certainly useful, but it's quite a job to pick out all the references you really need to get yourself up and running. Then there is the need to synthesize, integrate, and put all this information together in a coherent and useable form. This is the toughest and most overlooked area by most business-related text books. This guidebook provides this important integration function for you.

Finally, the large multi-pound compendiums chock full of everything you ever wanted to know about business serve well as references but do a poor job as guides. They simply cover too much material, much of which is not needed at the starting point of your business.

Every business has a life cycle that goes something like this:

1. Genesis of an idea
2. Get serious (real planning)
3. Startup
4. Growth
5. Build/diversify
6. Pass along (sell, get children involved)

This book focuses on the first three items of the list. The growth and build/diversify phases generally include an exercise in procuring additional capital for the business, which is a subject that has been treated extensively in many excellent books.

This is the book for you if you are considering starting a business and want an easy-to-use guide that will answer a good share of your questions AND provide clear references to other available materials when you need more specific information.

This book does not provide advice on how to "get rich quick." In fact, your business goal should not be to get rich ... Your goal should be to provide a product or service people want or need by operating an efficient and honest business. The result of this effort is likely to provide you wealth.

If you have any comments or corrections, please let us know.

Information International
Box 579, Great Falls, VA 22066
(703) 450-7049 voice;
(703) 450-7394 FAX
E-mail: bobs@isquare.com

For up-to-date small business information visit the award winning Small Business Advisor website on the Internet at http://www.isquare.com

To subscribe to The Small Business Advisor e-mail newsletter, send an e-mail to bobs@isquare.com with the word "subscribe" as the subject.

To business that we love we rise bedtime,
And go to't with delight.

... William Shakespeare

INTRODUCTION

Some of the material in this book is taken from business seminars presented by the author and includes many excellent ideas generated by exchanges with the attendees. The focus of the seminars is on learning from the mistakes of others. Statistics on business failure clearly show many mistakes are repeated over and over! It is our hope we can prevent you from repeating these mistakes.

The book is basically divided into areas we consider to be vital for business success:

- ✓ Focus Your Energy
- ✓ Choose Your Business with Care
- ✓ Choose a Partner Wisely
- ✓ Plan for Success and Failure
- ✓ Obtain the Right Professional Advice
- ✓ Establish a Banking Relationship
- ✓ Keep Home and Business Separate
- ✓ Market EVERY Day
- ✓ Protection
- ✓ Hire the Best (IF You Hire)
- ✓ Get Technology Smart
- ✓ Learn to Communicate

Most chapters contain references that will steer you to additional information. The references include specifics as to where to obtain the item, costs, and other relevant details. The same reference may be repeated in more than one chapter if it is relevant to the topic. An appendix is included that lists a variety of additional material that you will also find useful.

Throughout the text, many references are made to the U.S. Small Business Administration (SBA) publications. The easiest way to obtain these publications is to write to the SBA at Box 1000, Fort Worth, TX, 76119 and request a free copy of the "Directory of Business Development Publications." You may also contact your local SBA office whose number will be listed in the blue section of your local telephone directory under United States Government. The SBA also maintains a very informative Internet website at http://www.sba.gov

We suggest you quickly scan through all the chapters to get a feel for the content of each and then go back and read each chapter carefully. Use a highlighter and write your own personal notes in the margins. (We've provided a little extra "white space") Your personal notes will increase the book's value to you. Chapter 1, Prologue, briefly summarizes the contents of each chapter and appendix. Appendix VI is a glossary of small business terms to which you can refer for a unfamiliar word.

Lastly, we would like to comment on three excellent sources of information and help, the U.S. Small Business Administration (SBA) as noted above, one of its affiliates, the Service Corps of Retired Executives (SCORE), and the National Business Association (NBA).

1. The SBA provides a number of publications and videotapes that are very useful and are suggested throughout this book. They are informative and inexpensive, ranging in price from fifty cents to $2.00 for the publications and $30 for videotapes. The SBA also offers a loan guarantee program in conjunction with many banks throughout the nation. Details on this program can be obtained by

contacting the SBA. Reach the SBA at its toll-free telephone number (800) 827-5722, or look up their local number in the blue section of your telephone book.

2. SCORE, staffed by volunteers, provides free, impartial, and confidential counseling for entrepreneurs and has nearly 400 offices nationwide. To find the SCORE office nearest you, look in the blue section of your telephone book under Small Business Administration (they sponsor SCORE). Your local SCORE office conducts weekly or monthly workshops costing approximately $25, in which guest lecturers cover topics such as marketing, finance, market analysis, legal concerns, taxes, and insurance. These sessions are well worth your time and money. SCORE will also answer specific questions by e-mail. For additional details, visit their Internet page at: http://www.score.org

3. The NBA is a non-profit corporation whose charter is to provide assistance to small businesses. Their services and support include group health insurance, training programs, SBA loan assistance (as noted above), a credit union, discount buying, and travel discounts, just to name a few. Membership is currently $72 per year. Contact them for additional information and, if you have a computer (and you should have one!) ask for their free software which provides a detailed description of their services. The NBA can be reached at (800) 456-0440 or by writing to P.O. Box 870728, Dallas, TX 75287.

There is one thing stronger than all the armies in the world: an idea whose hour is come.

... Victor Hugo

CHAPTER 1 PROLOGUE

Planning and starting a business is a little like climbing a mountain. It is a perilous journey, fraught with unknown dangers and influences outside your control. But if you keep your goal in sight and plan very, very carefully, getting to the top can be a most rewarding experience. We'll revisit this metaphor later.

The statistics concerning survival rates of new businesses vary considerably depending on who's doing the reporting. For instance, the reported failure rate during the first three years ranges from 10% to 85%. The real figure is no doubt somewhere in between these limits. The point, however, is that considering there are nearly a million new business start-ups each year; many of them will fail. We're going to profit from these failures by learning the basis for the failures, adding this information to data we've gleaned from the successes, to give you a clear advantage. This guide contains a wealth of information that is based on many actual, hard-learned, and expensive lessons.

All the reasons for a business failure are too numerous to list, but they can be categorized into these major areas:

Lack of Entrepreneurial Qualities
Lack of Information
Lack of Planning

In the following chapters, we will discuss in some detail these areas and a number of others that relate closely to them. Sources of additional reference material are included at the end of each chapter.

Chapter 2 includes information that will allow you to assess your own entrepreneurial qualities. A checklist is included for you to test yourself.

Chapter 3 covers choosing your business and selecting its legal structure. The choice may seem obvious to you but you might be overlooking some obvious pitfalls. The "right" business can turn out to be a disaster if the choice is made for the wrong reasons. This chapter also discusses the numerous legal requirements of which you need to be aware.

Chapter 4 provides guidance on obtaining outside financing to start or expand your business.

Chapter 5 discusses partnerships and includes a checklist for choosing a partner who will be an asset to your business. An effective partnership can be a powerful combination for success, but the wrong partner is like stepping into the batter's box with two strikes against you.

Chapter 6 discusses planning. The lack of proper planning is the major reason for business failure. This chapter gives practical advice on the planning process, why it's important, and how to plan effectively for success. This chapter also covers planning for failure. Huh? Well, the facts are the facts ... Business is tough and failure is possible. If you plan ahead for the possibility of failure, you will be ready to deal with it.

Chapter 7 provides advice for working with accountants, attorneys, and insurance agents, all of whom you will be working with on a regular basis. Checklists are included for selecting and dealing with these professionals.

Chapter 8 covers the importance of a banking relationship, how to choose and deal with your bank. A listing of banking services is also included.

Chapter 9 discusses the significance of separation of home and business. It is no secret that many couples split up because of the pressures of one or the other going into business. Suggestions are listed that can prevent this tragedy.

Chapter 10 discusses marketing. This chapter is by no means comprehensive since marketing is a very complex arena, but what is offered are simple suggestions relative to basic marketing principles that can be critical to the long term health of your business. The appendix to this chapter contains listings for seeking out further information about marketing activities.

Chapter 11. Protection! Don't skim over this chapter! This very important area includes personal guarantee warnings, partnership agreements, and insurance.

Chapter 12 provides some ideas on hiring employees and suggests hiring may not be the best approach for you.

Chapter 13 discusses technology and its relation to your business. Computers and the Internet are discussed in some detail including selection of hardware and software; maintenance; security; and more. You will probably find early on that a computer is a necessary tool for your business.

Chapter 14 discusses the importance of the Internet. Information is included to show you how to "get connected." The Internet is becoming a very valuable information resource and marketing tool for small businesses.

Chapter 15 is about communications, writing and speaking. Included is a checklist for effective written and spoken communications.

Chapter 16 includes a listing of suggestions for day-to-day business operations, including important areas such as saving money and using the telephone to best advantage.

Chapter 17 provides a summary listing of the major items to be considered when starting and running your business and a few final thoughts.

Appendix I is a listing of reference material.

Appendix II is an index of the various checklists included throughout the text.

Appendix III contains information specific to home-based businesses.

Appendix IV is a listing of some useful Internet sites and reference material.

Appendix V provides information on obtaining a business merchant account so that your customers may pay for services and products with credit cards.

Appendix VI is a small business glossary.

Appendix VII is state specific small business contact information.

Each chapter of this guidebook contains useful information for both the first time business person and the more experienced entrepreneur. However, each chapter stands alone, and if you are looking for information on a specific topic, refer to the brief chapter descriptions above to determine what portion of the guidebook will be most useful for your specific situation.

CHAPTER 2
FOCUS YOUR ENERGY

(Entrepreneurial Qualities)

"AL, I'VE GOT TO ADMIRE YOUR ABILITY TO FOCUS ON YOUR WORK."

One of the major elements contributing to business failure is the lack of entrepreneurial qualities. So what are they? Do you fit the criteria? Don't put your head in the sand on this issue. Starting a business is tough and it is very important that you determine early on if you have the "right stuff." Better you find out now what qualities you may need to strengthen rather than finding out once it is too late.

John and I were recently discussing the problems he was having with his new business venture. After chatting for a while it was clear to me that he should have never undertaken the venture—He simply did not have the entrepreneurial 'spirit.' John didn't discuss his venture with me even though he knew I was a business consultant. He knew that I would tell him not to do it. You see, John KNEW he needed to strengthen certain qualities, but was blinded by the dollar signs in his eyes!

You need to be more honest with yourself than John, so let's take a little test. This test is an entrepreneurial aptitude test, a sort of "self-evaluation" checklist. A high score places you in the profile more likely to succeed in starting and operating a business. Answer each question honestly! We will then discuss each question. Grade each question on a scale of 0 to 5, with 5 being yes, absolutely, and 0 being no, absolutely.

CHECKLIST #1:
ENTREPRENEURIAL APTITUDE

☐ Are you a leader?

☐ Are you a high-energy person?

☐ Are you self-confident?

☐ Are you organized?

☐ Are you competitive?

☐ Are you prepared to work long hours, every day for an indefinite period?

☐ Do you have adequate resources?

☐ Are you in good health?

☐ Do you have a unique service or product?

☐ Is your spouse on board with your ideas?

☐ Are you willing to make short-term sacrifices in return for long term success?

☐ Are you a risk taker?

☐ Are you a good communicator?

☐ Do you have adequate experience?

Now total your score ... Good news, there is no failing score! The list only serves to provide an "awareness" of what you need to be thinking about. Now let's look into each question with a bit more care.

1. Are you a leader?

It is hard to "define" a leader, but it is easy to know one when you see one. A good "manager," by the way, is not necessarily a leader. It has been said that leading is doing the right thing and managing is doing things right! An entrepreneur must, of course, be a competent manager, but, more importantly, must lead the way to success.

A few years ago while consulting for a relay manufacturing business I met with the founder and owner. It was easy to see he was an excellent manager and organizer. He had effectively set up his company, found satis-factory help, and was quickly manufacturing small runs of high quality electromechanical relays. When he called me, the company was in trouble — Poor sales, decreasing order backlog, etc. The problem was determined to be that the market had been slowly moving towards solid-state relays and the electro-mechanical units simply were no longer being designed into equipment. In overlooking (or not being aware) of this fact, the owner, although a good manager, was not LEADING the company in a successful direction.

TRUISM 1

It takes a leader to successfully start, run, and grow a business.

A group of surveyors was lost in the jungle and had been wandering for a number of hours under the hot sun. They were following instructions from Harry, who was carefully organizing their route through the dense jungle underbrush. He made sure they were not going in circles, assigned one member of the party to keep the long knifes sharpened that they carried to cut the brush, ensured rest breaks were periodically taken, that water was being rationed, and so forth. Finally, Paul, nearly exhausted and anxious to end this adventure, climbed a tall tree, took a look, and yelled down to the group, "Hey, we're going the wrong direction, there's a town about 200-yards off to the left!" Harry was a good manager, but Paul is a leader!

To be a good leader you must focus your energy. If you are going to start a business, be prepared to focus on your objectives. If you feel you lack leadership qualities, read one or more of the many good books available on the subject. No one really knows if a leader is born or made, but it is possible to focus on those qualities that most leaders seem to possess. The reference section at the end of this chapter suggests some reading material on this subject.

2. Are you a "high energy" person?

Starting and running a business requires considerable energy and the ability to focus on your objectives. Long hours will be required which, if you are already employed full time, quickly takes its toll. A high-energy level is a must.

If you know in your heart that you're a ball of fire, but just can't get off the couch in the evenings, you might want to look into your diet and exercise programs.

Note at what times of day you are at your best. Some of us are "morning people" and others are "night people." A morning person might not do well running a business that requires late hours and conversely, a night person should not consider an early morning delivery business!

3. Are you self-confident?

You must believe in what you are doing. Get involved in something you are GOOD at doing. Familiarity and ability breed confidence. Don't make the mistake of getting into a business because it looks like a good money maker or it is the "business of choice" this year. If you know absolutely nothing about the restaurant business, don't start a restaurant!

If your business encompasses one or more of your hobbies or other long-term interests and/or expertise, your self-confidence will be enhanced. Your level of confidence is important ...You must believe in what you are doing and be confident of attaining your business goals.

4. Are you organized?

You need to be organized in order to make good use of your time. Rest assured, you will never have all the time you think you need to accomplish what you feel needs to be done, but organization allows you to use time in the most effective manner. In other words, you will get more done in less time. How organized are you?

> Do you get things done on time ... always?
> Can you always find what you're looking for?
> Do you keep a schedule? A "to-do" list?
> Are you on time for appointments?

If you "feel" organized, you probably are. If you need some improvement, start by keeping a detailed schedule of your activities. Refer to references at end of this chapter for suggested information resources on this topic.

5. Are you competitive?

From day one on, you and your business will be in competition. A competitive spirit is almost mandatory. Are you competitive? Do you strive to be first or the best? Your hobbies and sporting interests can tell you a lot about your competitive nature. You are your own best judge. Give it some thought ... If you're a fighter, your chances for success are improved.

6. Are you prepared to work long hours?

During a recent lecture I asked the participants why they were contemplating starting their own business. One of the people in the audience responded by saying she was tired of being required by her supervisor to frequently work late. She wanted her own business so that she could have more free time and work her own hours.

There's an old joke that says an entrepreneur only works half time ... 12 hours a day. The fact is, 12 hours a day might be a little light. Building and operating your own business is considerably more time intensive then working for someone else. You can set your own hours all right ... From about 6AM to midnight! The typical entrepreneur does, like the old joke, work an average of 12 hours per day, six and sometimes seven days a week. However, this hard work can bring rewards and a feeling of accomplishment like nothing else can.

7. Do you have adequate resources?

 Have you thought out what kind of monetary investment will be required? Do you have it? Can you borrow it? Lack of adequate resources is one of the major causes of business failure.

TRUISM 2

Your business is likely to operate at a loss
for the first year of operation.

There are many excellent references that provide details about resources required and where and how to borrow what you need. The following list will give you a few preliminary guidelines to keep in mind:

- Prepare a listing of start-up costs and first year expenses. Assume NO sales will be made and that you will be operating at a loss. You should have this much capital available the day you open your door for business. These expenses include, but are not limited to, items such as equipment, office supplies, deposits for utilities, legal fees, licenses, advertising, operating cash, wages, repairs, shipping, rent, utilities, insurance, and taxes. Many of these expenses can be reduced or eliminated if your business is conducted from your own residence.

- If your personal financial resources are not adequate, line up other sources before the cash is required. Don't forget to obtain formal commitments.

TRUISM 3

A personal guarantee will probably be required if you borrow money from a bank.

- Think very carefully about personal guarantees before you decide it is worth the risk. Chapter 11 has more details on this important topic.

• Remember that most investors are more likely to invest in an entrepreneur that puts up some personal cash than one who is looking for 100% financing.

8. Are you in good health?

You're likely to be working hard, long hours and you need to be in good shape. This is not a trivial matter ... You need to look after yourself. If you are not already into an exercise program ... Start! If you smoke ... Quit! If you are a heavy drinker ... ease off. Take a stress management course to be prepared when it hits ... and it will.

9. Do you have a unique service or product?

Almost too obvious to even mention but amazingly enough, forgotten by many. Your product or service need not be "new" in the sense of "never before available." But it must be unique in the sense of providing better service, better support, or a new approach.

Dave, a good friend and fellow amateur radio operator, started a radio equipment and accessory retail store. Certainly not new, since there are hundreds of such stores throughout the country and, in fact, there were three within 50 miles of Dave's location. However, in less than a year, he was outselling the other two stores and had acquired a good share of their former customers. Why? Dave knew he needed to provide something unique that would make his store more useful than his competitors. Knowing that communications were "going digital" and there was a high interest in combining computers and radio equipment, Dave provided custom software to marry the customer's computer with the radio equipment he sold. He's still going strong.

TRUISM 4

In order to be successful, your business must provide a service or product that people want to buy.

10. Is your family on board with your ideas?

Will you have the support of your significant other? Trouble at home is the last thing you need when starting a business. The statistics in this area are grim ... a lot of breakups occur during and immediately after a new business start-up. Don't let this happen to you ... talk it out first. Make sure you share common goals and objectives.

11. Are you willing to make short term sacrifices in return for long term success?

This may be obvious but think it through just the same. You may be spending less time with family and friends, taking fewer (if any) vacations, probably not wearing the latest fashions or driving a new car. All of these things, we hope, are temporary but a lot of people are simply not willing to give them up. If you can't, reconsider your priorities before making a decision that may not be right for you.

12. Are you a risk taker?

You need to be! Starting a business can be a big risk and you need to be able to make risky decisions and cope with the consequences. Taking risks is commonplace with the entrepreneur ... opportunity comes with risk.

A few years back, I gave up a government job, and moved to Venezuela to start a business with partners from that country. I didn't speak the language nor was I familiar with the legal system. I was in a strange country, not understanding the language, and was dependent upon my partners to get business. The venture turned out to be successful after some quick learning experiences, but it certainly was a risk. I still remember my friends saying to me, "You're giving up your government job for what??" Risk? Yes! But what an experience!

My example above is an extreme one, but you get the idea. If you think what I did is completely crazy, you may not be a risk taker yourself. (Of course, personal situations play a big part in these kinds of decisions but it's the mental attitude we're interested in here.)

There is risk of some sort in just about every decision you make but your business decisions (Should I hire another worker? Should I purchase that machine? Should I sign the contract?) carry major financial consequences and in some cases can spell life or death for your company. Someone who is somewhat comfortable with taking risk is more likely to make the decision that will result in the bigger payoffs. Those kinds of decisions can spell growth for your company.

13. Are you a good communicator?

Strong writing and speaking skills are essential to selling your product or service and yourself. Be honest here; if you need improvement, take a writing or public speaking course at your local university and visit your library for books on the subject. Consider joining Toastmasters, for example, or take a Dale Carnegie course. Consider enrolling in a correspondence course.

14. Do you have the necessary experience?

You should start your business in an area where you have both an interest and experience. Don't get involved in something you know little about ... it's a strike against you that you do not need. Mind you, you don't have to be an expert in everything - in fact, you can't be. For example, you can always hire professional help in the area of marketing, finance, and taxes. If you lack some of the technical expertise required,   you   might   consider   a partnership with someone who will complement your expertise. Make sure this person shares your goals and objectives. Chapter 5 includes information about selecting a partner.

Some so called "experts" have written that a real entrepreneur should not care what business he or she is in since "business is business." Not so! As an entrepreneur, you want the best odds for success. You should get involved only with something you are both good at and interested in.

she is in since "business is business." Not so! As an entrepreneur, you want the best odds for success. You should get involved only with something you are both good at and interested in.

Now that you have a better idea of the meaning of each of the "entrepreneurial elements," go back and review the marks you gave yourself in the test and adjust them if necessary. If you still feel you need to improve in any area, consider some of the suggestions in the chart on the following page which suggests ways in which you can improve.

SUMMARY

It is important that you understand the qualities that most successful entrepreneurs have and take steps to strengthen those in which you are weak. An honest assessment of yourself is essential. When you're satisfied and know you are ready, get your business started NOW ... or someone else will!

TRUISM 5

A really good idea will not last for long before someone else runs with it.

ELEMENT	SUGGESTION TO IMPROVE
Leadership	Take leadership seminars Read books on the subject Practice leadership in every situation
High-Energy, Health	Start a regular exercise program Eat right, quit smoking, drink lightly Get involved in sports ... Stay active!
Self-confidence	Join a club and run for an office Write an article about your hobby Give a speech to a group Read books available on the subject Listen to motivational cassette tapes
Organization	Start a daily "to do" listing Clean up your working area Start a "tickler" file Carry a notebook & pen at all times
Competitiveness	Get involved in a sport Enter a public speaking contest
Long Hours, Hard Work	This one's up to you! Remember long hours WILL be required for success
Resources	Assess your financial situation Prepare a net-worth summary
Unique Product or Service	Conduct market research Reassess your product/service Talk to your competition Subscribe to and read trade journals
Family Involvement	Talk about your ideas Come to an understanding before you start the business
Sacrifice	Nothing you can do about this one except to understand what it means
Risk Taker	This one's up to you!
Communicating	Join Toastmasters Give speeches at every opportunity Take a course in writing & speaking Practice writing at every opportunity
Experience	Enroll in courses at local colleges Work for your competition for a while Attend trade shows in your area Subscribe to trade magazines Attend SCORE meetings

REFERENCES

ITEM	"Leadership is an Art" by Max Depree
DESCRIPTION	Published by Dell. Excellent text on leadership.
WHERE TO OBTAIN	Bookstores, Library

ITEM	"On Becoming a Leader" by W. Bennis
DESCRIPTION	Published by Addison-Wesley.
WHERE TO OBTAIN	Bookstores, Library

ITEM	"Principle-Centered Leadership" by Stephen Covey
DESCRIPTION	Published by Summit Books. (Hardback). A lot of good ideas and relevant information.
WHERE TO OBTAIN	Bookstores, Library

ITEM	"Super-Leadership" by Manz & Sims, Jr.
DESCRIPTION	Published by Berkeley Books. Discusses teaching others to become leaders.
WHERE TO OBTAIN	Bookstores, Library

ITEM	"Getting Organized" by Stephanie Winston
DESCRIPTION	Published by Warner Books, 1978. Organization techniques.
WHERE TO OBTAIN	Bookstores, Library

Fortune favors the bold

... Virgil

CHAPTER 3
GETTING STARTED

"BECAUSE OF YOUR DEDICATION AND HARD WORK THIS PAST WEEK, WE'RE AWARDING YOU WITH A 3-DAY WEEKEND."

So you've decided you have the right stuff to be an entrepreneur and you're anxious to get that new idea off the ground. Now let's ponder some of the other considerations you'll need to look at. This chapter will give you some recommendations about choosing a business that is right for you. Then we'll look at the advantages and disadvantages of the types of business legal structures (sole proprietorships, partnerships, corporations). The last section looks at some of the legal requirements that can add to the complexity of the process and of which you need to be aware before you open your doors for business.

START, BUY, OR FRANCHISE?

There are basically three ways to begin a business. You can start your own, purchase an existing business, or invest in a franchise operation. There are good reasons for each choice and each carries its own advantages and risks. Most of us, however, will start our own because of the (usually) small initial investment required. Purchasing an existing business or a franchise can require a significant capital investment. The information in this and other chapters is applicable regardless of the method you choose for starting your business.

A detailed discussion of buying an existing business or a franchise is beyond the scope of this book but considerable literature is available, some of which is listed in the reference section at the end of this chapter. However, a few words of caution are in order. You should have help from an attorney and accountant who have experience with business purchases. Do not do it alone no matter how good the deal looks or how much pressure is being applied for you to "close the deal." *Caveat Emptor* ("let the buyer beware") is what to remember when considering any purchase and especially if it's a franchise.

There are thousands of franchise opportunities, many of which are simply too good to be true. Be cautious and get educated before you make any decisions. Whether purchasing a business or franchise, the best advice is to investigate EVERYTHING with great care. Once you have signed on the dotted line, it's almost always too late for second thoughts. If you are considering a franchise, look into the information that is available from the following sources:

International Franchise Association (IFA). 1350 New York Avenue, NW, Washington, DC 20005. (202) 628-8000. Numerous books and pamphlets are available ranging in price from $1.00 to $225.00.

US Government Printing Office. Superintendent of Documents, Washington, DC 20402. (202) 512-1800. "The Franchise Opportunities Handbook." $21.00. Ask for document #00300900649-0. You may pay with a credit card.

Federal Trade Commission (FTC). Bureau of Consumer Protection, Washington, DC 20580. (202) 326-2970. Free brochures covering franchise opportunities and questions and answers about franchise operations.

CHOOSING A BUSINESS.

The fact that you're reading this book says that you probably want to own and operate a business. In all likelihood you also have a good idea of what that business will be. We'll give you some help to ensure you've selected the business that's right for you.

TRUISM 6

Your business success will be directly proportional to how much you love what you are doing.

Considering the amount of effort you will need to expend as an entrepreneur to make your venture successful, the business you select should be something you love. There are lots of reasons why people choose to start a new business. At the top of the list is dissatisfaction with their present job. If this is your situation, try to understand why you don't like your present job. This will help you select a business that will be right for you.

Select a business because you have something to give, because you understand the market and because you know you are going to do a better job than anyone else. Don't pick one because you want to make a quick buck or because the "deal looks just too good to pass up." If your heart and soul are in the business, you have a much better chance of being successful.

The business you choose should fit with realistic goals and an honest assessment of yourself. The following checklist will help you decide on a business that can be successful for you.

> Bruce bought a fast food franchise because the opportunity looked too good to pass up. It might have been, but Bruce knew nothing about the food or restaurant business, and as far as I knew, didn't even like fast food! Care to guess how successful he was? Or how long it lasted? Care to guess what happened even though "all the details are taken care of for you?"

CHECKLIST #2: CHOOSING A BUSINESS

☐ Is this the kind of work I really enjoy?

Look to your current interests. Many successful small businesses grow out of hobbies because a hobby is chosen for all the right reasons ... you enjoy the task, the challenge, the time spent.

☐ Do I have the required technical expertise?

Don't get involved in a business if you know little or nothing about it. The story related above is a true one ... and one of many like it. When you have the necessary technical expertise, you can ask the right questions, make good business decisions and assess other "expert" opinions.

☐ Can I make enough money in this business?

First, your financial goals should be realistic. Then look around at similar businesses to see how they are doing. Talk to the owners. Most will give you enough information for you to decide if it's right for you financially. This will help you to pick a business that can satisfy your financial goals.

☐ Can I get the help I will need?

If your business is not going to be a one-person operation, you need to find out if the right kind of help is available in your immediate area. Are there similar businesses in the area? Also check with local employment agencies.

☐ Do I understand the market?

Will you be able to find customers? Do you have the knowledge required to set prices appropriately? Will you be able to direct a marketing program? (You might not do this yourself, but you may have to manage the effort).

CHOOSING THE BUSINESS LEGAL STRUCTURE

Okay, you've chosen your business. What next? No doubt, one of the most asked questions by the prospective business owner is "Should I incorporate?" To answer this question, we need to examine what the options are and their respective advantages and disadvantages. So as not to keep you in suspense, it should be noted that most new small businesses will not incorporate — but will operate as a sole proprietorship.

Actually, you have three basic business structures from which to choose:

1. Sole proprietorship
2. Partnership (limited or general)
3. Corporation (S, C or LLC)

TRUISM 7

There is no "best choice" for a
business structure.

The legal structure you choose depends on a number of things, including your type of business, individual situation, goals for the business, and a number of other personal and financial factors. Before deciding what's best for you, discuss your plans with your accountant and attorney. Make sure you are prepared to describe your business plans in some detail. It will be money and time well spent. Making the right choice can help you avoid a mistake that can cost you big in terms of possible future liability (See Chapter 7, Get Professional Advice).

Before you have any discussions with your professional advisors, it is useful to understand the basics of the various legal structures available to you ... sole proprietorship, partnership, and various forms of corporations.

SOLE PROPRIETORSHIP

This is the most popular form of small business and, as the name implies, ownership is totally vested with one person. It is the easiest to establish since no legal formalities are necessary. The only business requirement may be a license from your local jurisdiction to allow you to conduct the type of business you are planning. For example, you may need a license to sell food to the public.

Sole Proprietorship Advantages:

1. Easy and quick and usually the least expensive to establish.

2. You have total ownership and control of the business.

3. All the profits of the business belong to you, the owner.

4. No additional Federal taxation on business profits (No double taxation).

5. No periodic business reporting to the IRS or other government agency is required.

6. Income tax filing is simply part of your annual personal tax return (Schedule C).

Sole Proprietorship Disadvantages:

1. The owner is personally liable for all business debts and the liability is not limited

to the value of the business. <u>You are personally liable</u> for any and all business debt you incur.

2. It is generally more difficult to borrow money or obtain outside investment than with other types of legal structures.

3. If the owner is incapacitated for any reason, the business is likely to fail.

4. All management responsibility is with the owner which can be a heavy burden.

5. You must pay self-employment tax on the business net income.

IMPORTANT NOTE

A "home business" is frequently a sole proprietorship and offers a number of unique advantages. However, just because you are conducting business from your home does not exempt you from possible legal or other liabilities. See Appendix III for a listing of the advantages of a home-based business.

PARTNERSHIP

This type of business is just what the name implies: Business ownership is divided between two (or more) partners. The general partnership is the most common and is formed to conduct a business with two or more partners being fully involved in the operation of the business. All the partners share both profits and liabilities. A limited partnership, as the name implies, provides for limited liability of the partners. (This liability can be no greater than the partner's investment in the partnership). In a limited partnership there must be a least one general partner who remains liable for all the debts of the partnership.

Forming a partnership is complex and legal advice is very important. The kind of partnership and the type of partner you will be determines your potential personal liability.

Partnership Advantages:

1. Synergy as a result of pooling partners' different areas of expertise.

2. The partnership does not pay Federal income taxes. An informational tax return (IRS Form 1065) must be filed which shows the pass-through of income/loss to each partner.

3. Liability may be spread among the partners.

4. Investment can come from the partners in the form of a loan which creates interest income for the partners and a business deduction for the partnership.

Partnership Disadvantages:

1. Formation and subsequent changes in structure are complex.

2. Problems with partner(s) as the result of misunderstandings, different goals, etc., can weaken or destroy the partnership.

3. Limited partners are liable for debt if they are active managers in the business. General partners have unlimited liability. You may

also be liable for the commitments of your partners.

CORPORATION

There are three major types of corporations, the C-corporation ("regular corporation"), the S-corporation (or "S-Corp"), and the Limited Liability Corporation (or "LLC"). All of these forms of the corporation are complex legal entities. Their detailed structure may vary from state to state (incorporating a business in a given state allows you to conduct business only in that state). It is essential for you to obtain legal advice if you are thinking about forming a corporation. (See Chapters 7 and 11). Since each state has its own set of corporation laws, you should contact the appropriate state office in your state (usually the office of the Secretary of State) for additional material and procedures. A listing of these offices for all 50 states is included at the end of this chapter. Most offices can provide a guide for new businesses to follow for incorporation and doing business in their state. Call or write for a copy.

Most people immediately think of incorporating in order to minimize their personal liability. Indeed, the liability of stockholders (owners) in a corporation is limited under certain and complex conditions. Today, with the Tax Reform Act of 1986 and other legislation, there are really few good tax reasons to incorporate (with the exception of dividing corporate profits as noted below). The best reason for incorporating is, in fact, the limited liability. However, there is no such thing as total insulation from liability resulting from doing business as a corporation.

Record keeping and tax matters with a corporation are difficult and time-consuming tasks usually requiring the services of an accountant. You need to keep this in mind when considering operating costs for your business.

Avoid the "do it yourself" incorporation guides. Incorporating is a complex process and you should not take on the task yourself. You cannot afford any mistakes at this point in your new business, so if you decide incorporation is for you, do it right and spend the money required to have it done professionally. Legal fees for setting up a corporation can run between $350 and $1,500 (assuming it is relatively straightforward). See Chapter 7.

REGULAR CORPORATION

The corporation is a taxable entity and, as such, pays taxes. This results in the "double taxation" you may have heard about. The corporation pays corporate taxes on its profits, and then, you the owner (shareholder), pay personal taxes on the dividends your corporation pays you. (The dividends are not deductible by the corporation). This is one of the biggest disadvantages of a corporation.

On the other hand, incorporating your business usually makes it easier to establish credit with suppliers and borrow from banks. If you expect to use outside investors for business capital, a corporation is a must.

Regular Corporation Advantages:

1. Shareholders (the owners) enjoy personal limited liability.

2. It is generally easier to obtain business capital than with other legal structures.

3. Profits may be divided among owners and the corporation in order to reduce taxes by taking advantage of lower tax rates.

4. The corporation does not dissolve upon the death of a stockholder (owner) or if ownership changes.

5. Favorable tax treatment for employee fringe benefits including medical, disability, and life insurance plans.

6. 70% of any dividends received by the corporation from stock investments are deductible (unless you purchased the stock with borrowed money).

Regular Corporation Disadvantages:

1. More expensive and complex to set up than other legal structures.

2. Completing tax returns usually requires the help of an accountant.

3. Double taxation on profits paid to owners (corporation pays corporate taxes on profits and owner pays personal taxes on dividends from the corporation).

4. Recurring annual corporate fees.

5. Tax rates are higher than individual rates for profits greater than approximately $75,000.

6. 28% accumulated earnings tax on profits in excess of $250,000.

7. Business losses are not deductible by the corporation.

S-CORPORATION

The S-corporation offers the limited liability advantages of a corporation but does NOT pay Federal taxes. All the earnings and losses of an S-corporation are passed through to the shareholders. It is a popular form of incorporation in the startup years of a business but there are some subtle disadvantages that need to be taken into account as you grow. Again, because of the complexities involved, talk with your attorney and accountant.

S-corporation Advantages:

1. Owners enjoy personal limited liability as in a regular corporation.

2. No Federal income tax liability, and in most cases, no state income tax.

3. Profit/losses are passed to owners ... no double taxation.

4. The S-corporation does not dissolve if one of the owners dies or otherwise leaves (like a regular corporation).

5. Wholly owned subsidiaries are permitted.

S-corporation Disadvantages:

1. Legal assistance is required to set up.

2. Maximum of 75 shareholders.

3. Only one class of common stock is permitted (no preferred stock).

LIMITED LIABILITY CORPORATION (LLC)

This type of corporation blends the tax advantages of a partnership and the limited liability advantages of a corporation. Owners of an LLC are referred to as "members." As you might expect, it also has some limitations but is definitely worth considering. Ask about the LLC when you contact your appropriate state office for incorporation information as suggested earlier in the chapter.

LLC Advantages:

1. Limited personal liability for the owners (like a corporation and unlike a partnership).

2. No Federal taxes (like a partnership).

3. No limit on the number of stockholders (unlike an S-corporation).

4. More than one class of stock is permitted (unlike an S-corporation).

5. Business losses may be deducted on your personal tax return (like a S-corporation).

LLC Disadvantages:

1. Legal assistance is required to set up. The paperwork is complex.

2. No "continuity of life" as in a regular corporation. The LLC dissolves if one of the owners dies or otherwise leaves. However, other formal agreements between the owners can overcome this.

3. Some states require than an LLC have more than one member.

MAKING YOUR CHOICE

As already noted, it is difficult to give specific advice as to the choice of legal business structure since every situation will be unique. The advantages and disadvantages noted above should be assessed based on your particular situation. In any case, it is important to discuss your plans with advisors including both an attorney and an accountant prior to making your final decision. The various tax consequences for corporations and partnerships are complex and must be carefully considered for each specific situation.

When discussing your plans with your advisors, keep in mind the following points:

- The LLC is well worth looking into.

- Saving taxes is one of most important reasons to consider when selecting your structure. Keep in mind that there are generally few tax advantages with a corporation if your total taxable business income is more than $75,000.

- Don't select the corporation structure based on possible tax advantages of profit-sharing plans since the Keogh, SEP, and IRA plans available to a sole proprietorship are equally beneficial.

- If you consider a partnership, be certain to have a complete partnership agreement drawn up by your attorney. (See Chapter 5).

- Consider a S-corporation if you expect business losses for the first year or two of your business. These losses can be passed through to the owners as tax relief whereas they provide no current benefit in a regular corporation.

OTHER REQUIREMENTS

There are a number of other items that must be addressed when starting your business regardless of its structure and type. Before conducting any business activity, review the following listing lest you get yourself into legal trouble or, at the very least, become liable for various fines. Once again, it is a good idea to review these items with your attorney and get help where required.

- Business licenses and permits.

   Depending on your type of business, Federal, state, county, and local business licenses and/or permits may be required. It is impossible to list all the specific requirements by business or jurisdiction. You should first check on your state's requirements by contacting the appropriate state office or agency. (See the listing at end of this chapter). They may also be able to assist you with the local, and possibly the Federal requirements. Then check with your local city or county government offices (usually in the courthouse) for information about local requirements. Don't overlook this, since heavy fines are usually associated with conducting a business without proper licenses and permits.

- Business name.

   Give some careful thought to the name of your business. You should select more than one possibility since you may not be able to use your first choice. You cannot and should not use a name already in use. Most states will allow you to "reserve" your desired name for a short period of time in order to allow you to complete other required paperwork. The state office can tell you if your selected name is in use and suggest you pick another one, if necessary. You should also check with your local county clerk to see if the name you picked is being used locally. In any case, you do not want your business name confused with another for a variety of obvious reasons. Some states require you register for a "fictitious name" if the name of your business is something other than your own full legal name (e.g., "Robert Sullivan Consulting Services"). The cost to register varies but is generally between $10 and $100. Check with your local government for specific requirements.

• Tax payments.

You will be required to make periodic estimated Federal and sometimes state tax payments regardless of your business legal structure. The requirements vary and you should discuss the matter with your accountant. Don't be late in filing since penalties accrue.

• Various IRS reporting requirements.

There are a large number of IRS reporting requirements that you need to be aware of since penalties can be severe. These include such requirements as the filing of different types of Form 1099 for payments to individuals and reporting different kinds of income. It is very important for you to discuss what requirements must be met with your accountant.

The checklist on the following page taken from IRS publication #334 (Rev. Nov 91), will give you an idea of the Federal tax requirements for various business legal structures.

- Collection of sales tax.

  If your business will be selling goods to end-user customers (the public), it is likely you will have to collect sales tax for the state and/or local government. Check with your local government offices on this one ... every state is different. You will probably have to apply for a sales tax identification number that will identify you to the local and state government as a seller of goods. The process is easy and usually no cost is involved. There can also be monthly reporting requirements.

You may be liable for	If you are:	Use Form	Due on or before
Income tax	Sole proprietor	Schedule C (1040)	Same day as 1040
	Individual (partner) or S corp shareholder	1040	15th day of 4th month after end of tax year
	Corporation	1120 or 1120-A	Same but 3rd month
	S corporation	1120S	Same but 3rd month
Self-employment tax	Sole proprietor, or individual who is a partner	Schedule SE (1040)	Same day as 1040
Estimated tax	Sole proprietor, or individual who is a partner or S corp shareholder	1040-ES	15th day of 4th, 6th, 9th mos of tax yr, and 15th day of 1st mo after end of tax yr
	Corporation	1120-W	15th day of 4th, 6th, 9th, 12th mo of tax yr
Annual return of income	Partnership	1065	15th day of 4th mo after end of tax yr
Social security & Medicare taxes (FICA) Withholding of income tax	Sole proprietor, corporation, S corp, or partnership	941	4/30, 7/31, 10/31, and 1/31
		8109 (for deposits)	
Providing info on social security and Medicare taxes (FICA) & the withholding of income tax	Sole proprietor, corporation, S corp, or partnership	W-2 (to employee)	1/31
		W-2, W-3 (to SSA)	Last day of Feb
Federal unemployment (FUTA) tax	Sole proprietor, corporation, S corp, or partnership	940-EZ or 940	1/31
		8109 (for deposits)	4/30, 7/31, 10/31, 1/31 if liability >$100
Info returns for payments to non employees & transactions with other persons	Sole proprietor, corporation, S corp, or partnership	Forms 1099: See IRS Pub #334, Chapter 37	1/31 to recipient and IRS by 2/28
Excise taxes	Sole proprietor, corporation, S corp, or partnership	See IRS Pub #334, Chapter 36	See instructions on the forms

The following checklist of business legal requirements is excerpted from "Starting & Operating a Business in [state]" and reprinted here with permission from The Oasis Press® and M. D. Jenkins. It provides an excellent summary of those items that need to be considered when starting a business in a specific state. (The chapter numbers shown in parenthesis refer to chapters in this guidebook where additional information on that item may be found.) Some of the material below duplicates the requirements listed in the IRS publication checklist shown above.

CHECKLIST #3:
NEW BUSINESS LEGAL REQUIREMENTS

☐ Obtain local business licenses.

☐ Check on local zoning ordinances, regulations, and other land use restrictions.

☐ Determine if your particular business requires a state license to operate (3).

☐ Determine if any Federal permit or license is required (3).

☐ Be prepared to make estimated income tax payments almost immediately after starting business or incorporating.

☐ Apply for a sales and use tax seller's permit if you will sell tangible personal property.

☐ File sales and use tax returns, if sales or use tax must be collected on your sales.

☐ File with the county clerk and "publish" a fictitious business name statement, if the business operates under a fictitious name, and then file an affidavit of publication with the county clerk (in most states).

☐ Locate a good insurance agent or retain and meet with an insurance consultant regarding fire, accident, liability, theft, and other types of commercial insurance you need. Then obtain the necessary insurance coverage (11).

☐ If you purchase real estate, you must withhold up to 10% of the purchase price and remit it to the IRS if the seller is a foreign individual or foreign owned company, under the Foreign Investment in Real Property Tax Act. Otherwise, you should insist upon receiving an affidavit that the seller is not a non-resident alien, with his or her taxpayer identification number, unless you are certain that he or she is a U.S. citizen or resident.

☐ For a sole proprietorship, report any self-employment income on Schedule SE of Federal Form 1040, and report income or loss on Schedule C of Form 1040.

☐ A partnership files Form 1065, to report partnership income. Each partner reports their portion of the partnership's income on Schedule SE of Form 1040 and income and loss from the partnership on Schedule E of Form 1040.

☐ For a limited partnership, file a Certificate of Limited Partnership with the Secretary of State and copies in counties where the partnership will have places of business or real estate (in most states).

☐ For a corporation, file articles of incorporation, adopt bylaws, and observe the necessary corporate formalities. File Federal income tax return Form 1120 (or 1120-S for an S-corp). If property is transferred to the corporation tax-free under IRS Section 351, report required information relating to the transfer on the corporation's income tax return for that year.

☐ For a corporation or a partnership, apply for a Federal Employer Identification Number on Form SS-4, even if the business has no employees.

☐ File annual tax information returns, Forms 1096 and 1099 series, for payments of $600 or more for items such as rent, interest, and compensation for services, and send 1099's to the payees. File Form 1098 for mortgage interest of $600 or more your business receives in a year from an individual. Also, report any cash payments or cash equivalents of more than $10,000 that you receive to the IRS within 15 days. Such filing may have to be done on computer-readable magnetic media.

☐ If your business is a corporation, be sure to obtain an adequate supply of Federal tax deposit coupons in time to make your estimated tax payments.

After reading over the previous list, you'll have a better understanding of why it's important to talk with both your attorney and accountant. Remember, also, that there may be additions to this list for certain states. You should check with your own state (see listing below) for specific compliance requirements necessary for your type of business. Also refer to Chapter 12 for additional requirements if you are going to hire employees.

STATE OFFICES FOR INCORPORATION INFORMATION:

Write or call the office in your state and request their guide or brochure covering corporation registration. The literature you receive will most likely contain other information about doing business in your state such as Federal Employer Identification Numbers (EIN), various tax liabilities, and other licenses and permits that may be required.

Also refer to Appendix VII, State Specific Information, which lists a number small business related organizations in each state.

ALABAMA	Secretary of State, State House, Room 208, Montgomery 36130-7701 (205) 242 5324
ALASKA	State Capital, P. O. Box C, Juneau 99811 (907) 465 2530
ARIZONA	Secretary of State, 1700 W. Washington, West Wing, Phoenix 85007 (602) 542 4285
ARKANSAS	Secretary of State, 256 State Capital Building, Little Rock 72201 (501) 682 3409
CALIFORNIA	Secretary of State, 1230 J. Street, Sacramento 95814 (916) 445 0620
COLORADO	Secretary of State, 1560 Broadway, Suite 200, Denver 80202 (303) 894 2200

CONNECTICUT	Secretary of State, State Capital, Hartford 06106 (203) 566 8827
DELAWARE	State Department, Townsend Bldg., Dover 19901 (302) 739 3073
DIST OF COL (DC)	Office of Business & Economic Development, 717 14th Street NW 20005 (202) 727 6600 for general business information and Corporation Division, D.C. Department of Consumer and Regulatory Affairs, 614 H. Street NW, Room 407, 20001. (202) 727 7278 for incorporation information.
FLORIDA	State Department, Plaza Level, Room 2, The Capital, Tallahassee 32399 (904) 488 3680
GEORGIA	Secretary of State, State Capital, Room 214, Atlanta 30334 (404) 656 2881
HAWAII	Business Registration Division, P.O. Box 40, Honolulu 96805 (808) 586 2820
IDAHO	Secretary of State, Statehouse, Room 203, Boise 83720 (208) 334 2300
ILLINOIS	Secretary of State, 213 Capital Bldg., Springfield 62756 (217) 785 3285
INDIANA	Secretary of State, Room 201, State House, Indianapolis 46204 (317) 232 6587
IOWA	Secretary of State, Statehouse, Des Moines 50319 (515) 281 7550

KANSAS	Secretary of State, 2nd Floor, Statehouse, Topeka 66612 (913) 296 2236
KENTUCKY	Secretary of State, Capital Bldg., Room 150, Frankfort 40601 (502) 564 2848
LOUISIANA	Secretary of State, P.O. Box 94125, Baton Rouge 70804 (504) 925 4716
MAINE	State Department, State House Station 148, Augusta 04333 (207) 289 4195
MARYLAND	Maryland Business Assistance Center, Department of Economic & Employment Development., 217 E. Redwood St., Baltimore 21202 (410) 767 1340
MASSACHUSETTS	Secretary of the Commonwealth, Room 337, State House, Boston (617) 727 2853
MICHIGAN	Corporation & Securities Bureau, 6546 Mercantile Way, Box 30222, Lansing 48909 (517) 334 6327
MINNESOTA	Secretary of State, 180 State Office Building, St. Paul 55155 (612) 296 9215
MISSISSIPPI	Secretary of State, P.O. Box 136, Jackson 39205 (601) 359 1350
MISSOURI	Secretary of State, P.O. Box 778, Jefferson City 65102 (314) 751 4194
MONTANA	Secretary of State, Room 225, State Capital, Helena 59620 (406) 444 3665
NEBRASKA	Secretary of State, 2300 State Capital Bldg., Lincoln 68509 (402) 471 4079

NEVADA	Secretary of State, Capital Complex, Carson City 89710 (702) 687 5203
NEW HAMPSHIRE	Secretary of State, Room 204, State House, Concord 03301 (603) 271 3244
NEW JERSEY	State Dept., State Capital Bldg., CN300, Trenton 08625 (609) 984 1900
NEW MEXICO	Secretary of State, Executive Legislature Bldg., Santa Fe 87503 (505) 827 3616
NEW YORK	State Dept., 162 Washington Avenue, Albany 12231 (518) 474 6200
NORTH CAROLINA	Secretary of State, 300 N. Salisbury St., Raleigh 27611 (919) 733 4161
NORTH DAKOTA	Secretary of State, 600 E. Boulevard, Bismark 50505 (701) 224 2900
OHIO	Secretary of State, E. Broad St., 14th Floor, Columbus 43266, (614) 466 1145
OKLAHOMA	Secretary of State, 101 State Capital Bldg., Oklahoma City 73105 (405) 521 3048
OREGON	Corporation Division, 158 12th St., NE, Salem 97310 (503) 378 4166
PENNSYLVANIA	State Dept., North Office Building, Harrisburg 17120 (717) 787 1978
RHODE ISLAND	Secretary of State, Room 218, State House, Providence 02903 (401) 277 3040

SOUTH CAROLINA	Secretary of State, P.O. Box 11350, Columbia 29211 (803) 734 2158
SOUTH DAKOTA	Secretary of State, 500 E. Capital, Pierre 57501 605) 773 4845
TENNESSEE	Secretary of State, State Capital, 1st Floor, Nashville 37243 (615) 741 0529
TEXAS	Secretary of State, P.O. Box 12887, Austin 78711 (512) 463 5586
UTAH	Commerce Dept., P.O. Box 45802, Salt Lake City 84145 (801) 530 6027
VERMONT	Secretary of State, 26 Terrace St., Montpelier 05609 (802) 828 2371
VIRGINIA	State Corporation Commission, POB 1197, Richmond 23209 (804) 371 9733
WASHINGTON	Secretary of State, Legislative Bldg., AS-22, Olympia 98504 (206) 753 2896
WEST VIRGINIA	Secretary of State, State Capital Bldg., Charleston 25305 (304) 345 4000
WISCONSIN	Secretary of State, P.O. Box 7808, Madison 53707 (608) 266 3590
WYOMING	Secretary of State, State Capital, Cheyenne 82002 (307) 777 7311

SUMMARY

Choose your business with care and do it for the right reasons. You will be working hard at your new venture and love of your work is important. Obtain professional advice before selecting a sole proprietorship, partnership, or corporate structure for your business. Ask your advisors questions such as:

1. What legal structure is best for me? Why?

2. What is my worst case personal liability?

3. How complicated is it to form this structure? How much will it cost?

4. What is required in terms of Federal and state tax returns?

5. What are the tax consequences for me personally?

6. How will the structure affect hiring of personnel?

7. How will the structure affect the raising of capital?

Finally, do not begin any business activities until your business legal structure has been formalized and you've attended to the requirements discussed in the previous sections.

REFERENCES

ITEM	"Tax Guide for Small Business" IRS Publication #334
DESCRIPTION	Great guide! Get a copy.
WHERE TO OBTAIN	IRS Offices nationwide
COST	Free
COMMENTS	This publication is updated yearly. Also get a copy of Publication #509, "Tax Calendars for <current year>."

ITEM	"Selecting the Legal Structure for Your Firm" MP 25
DESCRIPTION	Provides brief descriptions of the various legal structures that a small businesses can use.
WHERE TO OBTAIN	U.S. Small Business Administration (SBA) P.O. Box 1000 Fort Worth, TX 76119 (800) 827-5722
COST	$1.00

ITEM	"Buying a Business for Very Little Cash" by Joseph R. Mancuso & Douglas D. Germann
DESCRIPTION	Evaluating the purchase of a franchise.
WHERE TO OBTAIN	Prentice-Hall, 15 Columbus Circle, New York, New York 10023

ITEM	"Starting and Operating a Business in (state)"
DESCRIPTION	Federal and state laws affecting businesses. Samples of government forms and where to obtain assistance. Sections on business legal forms, buying an existing business, starting and operating a business. A book for each state.
WHERE TO OBTAIN	PSI Research, Inc., 300 North Valley Drive, Grants Pass, OR 97526 (800) 228 2275 FAX (503) 476 1479
COST	$21.95
COMMENTS	Highly recommended, Complete up-to-date reference. Includes information on buying existing businesses and franchise operations .

ITEM	"Franchise Bible: A Comprehensive Guide" by Erwin J. Keup
DESCRIPTION	A complete guide to franchising
WHERE TO OBTAIN	PSI Research, 300 North Valley Drive, Grants Pass, OR 97526 (800) 228 2275
COST	$19.95

CHAPTER 4
FINANCING YOUR BUSINESS

MIDDLETOWN BANK
— YOUR FRIENDLY BANK —

LOAN DEPT.

"NO, BUT HAVE A NICE DAY."

If it is at all possible, you should start your business without any funding beyond what you have available. Do this by starting slowly and in conjunction with present employment. Start your business by working evenings and weekends while keeping your present job as long as practicable. This way, if the business does not meet your expectations, you have not incurred debt and will still have a job!

However, depending on the nature of the business outside funding may be necessary. For example, expensive equipment or initial stock may be required. When determining your financing needs, remember that nearly everyone underestimates what is required, so be careful and do your planning accordingly. And of course, don't forget to factor in contingency — sickness, bad weather, equipment breakdown, etc. Anything that increases the time line to profits! Best you figure on a year before you see a profit. Here are some items to keep in mind when preparing your startup budget:

- Office equipment (Fax machine, computer)
- Production equipment (for manufacturing)
- Office or production furniture
- Office supplies
- Legal and CPA fees
- Insurance
- Business licenses or permits
- Lease deposits
- Remodeling costs
- Utility deposits (this can be quite large!)
- Salaries
- Shipping
- Advertising and promotion

and the big one ... contingency!

What you want to avoid is having to find additional financing during your startup phase. It is generally easier to obtain financing the first time around!

There are two major forms of business financing.

1. **DEBT FINANCING**. This simply means you get a loan from someone or somewhere and go into debt! You are obligated to repay the money.

2. **EQUITY FINANCING**. This involves "selling" a portion of your company to an outside investor. You have no obligation to repay the funds. In general, this type of funding is provided by venture capital firms.

The fact is, 99.99% of all small businesses will utilize debt financing since most "equity lenders" (venture capital companies) are interested in lending large amounts of money, generally a million dollars or more. Here we will only consider sources for obtaining debt financing for your venture.

For those of you interested in equity financing (venture capital), here are some suggestions for locating possible sources:

- The yellow pages under "venture capital companies."

- Venture Capital World Online on the internet located at: http://www.vcworld.com. They provide a direct database link between investors searching for opportunities and entrepreneurs in need of venture capital.

- The National Venture Capital Association in Arlington, VA at (703) 528 4370.

SOURCES FOR DEBT FINANCING

1. YOURSELF! (Savings) You are your own best "lender" if you have the savings. This approach can be quick and easy.

> **CAUTION**: Ensure you have adequate savings for both the business and other life contingencies.

2. FRIENDS and RELATIVES. If they believe in you and your idea, friends and relatives are sometimes willing to fund you. Choose this route with care and ensure you execute a formal loan document stating loan terms (interest, terms of repayment).

> **CAUTION**: Many friends have been lost and many relatives alienated because of a small business failure.

3. BANKS and CREDIT UNIONS. Many banks and credit unions (check with your own first and with you local chamber of commerce for alternate possibilities) will loan money for starting a small business. This approach will require that you present a formal plan to the bank showing justification for the amount you are borrowing.

4. THE SMALL BUSINESS ADMINISTRATION (SBA). Check out their website (http://www.sba.gov). Contrary to what many believe the SBA does NOT generally loan money directly but rather guarantees a loan (normally up to 90%). This can make it a lot easier to obtain a bank loan since the bank's risk is lowered considerably. The exception is that the SBA does provide direct loans to certain groups including Vietnam-era and disabled veterans and handicapped individuals. In general, the SBA will

not offer any assistance until you have been turned down for a loan by a commercial bank.

Most loans guaranteed through the SBA are between $25,000 and $750,000. However, there is a "microloan" program for amounts from a few hundred dollars up to $25,000.

5. VENDOR FINANCING. If your business is one that relies heavily on certain vendors, it may be possible to obtain financing through the vendor. After all, they want you to use their product and therefore have an interest in helping you be successful.

6. STATE. Some states have small business financing authorities that issue tax-exempt development bonds that can be used to finance land, buildings and equipment for manufacturing businesses. Check with your local government office for details.

7. HOME EQUITY LOAN. Interest rates for this kind of loan are generally quite low and the interest is fully deductible for the first $100,000 borrowed.

> **CAUTION**: You are placing your home on the line!

8. LIFE INSURANCE. Some types of life insurance policies (whole life and universal) have cash value which can be borrowed at very low interest rates. You are not obligated to pay this money back but if

you don't, your policy payout is reduced by the amount borrowed.

9. RETIREMENT PLANS. Some retirement plans (401K for example) allow you to borrow against vested benefits. Generally, up to 50% may be borrowed as long as this is less than $50,000.

> **CAUTION**: If you quit your employment, the loan must be repaid immediately. If you don't the amount borrowed is treated as an early distribution and is taxable.

10. GRANTS. Many foundations provide funding in the form of grants. Check "The Foundation Directory" at your local library or visit their website at http://fdncenter.org to find out what foundations may have an interest in your specific business idea. The Foundation Center may be reached at (212) 620-4230.

11. CREDIT CARDS. These should be used with care because of the excessively high rates of interest usually charged.

A FINAL NOTE. Remember that many of these loan ideas will require you to sign a personal guarantee. This means that regardless of what happens to your business, you are personally liable for the repayment of the loan amount. Think carefully before signing.

CHAPTER 5
CHOOSING A PARTNER

T he right business partner can extend your expertise, provide a second opinion when required, share the workload, and provide a synergy that you just can't get working alone. Two heads really can be better than one.

On the other hand the wrong choice in a partner can sink you! Many businesses fail simply due to friction between the partners, or the inability to get things done for a variety of reasons.

This chapter will provide you with some help in choosing the right partner.

I started a business some time ago with a friend who, like myself, was an electronics engineer. The product was an innovative telecommunications device. The partnership was a fiasco. Since we were both design engineers, we argued forever about the design and other product details. After much pain, we got the unit prototyped and were ready to do some marketing. Of course, neither of us had the slightest idea of how to market. Finally, we gave up ... Another great idea bites the dust. Why didn't I find a partner who had expertise in MARKETING? I knew I had to sell my product! I also knew that I had the expertise to design the item myself. So, while friendship is important, of what value was my friend as a partner?

TRUISM 8

A friend or family member does not necessarily make a good business partner.

In choosing the right partner you must consider a number of factors. If you chose your partner wisely you will share the risk and alleviate some of your anxiety that is part of going it alone. Here are some factors to consider when selecting your partner:

CHECKLIST #4: CHOOSING A PARTNER

☐ Does this person bring expertise I don't have to the business? The story above helps illustrate why this is important. It also illustrates why having the same expertise can cause difficulties.

☐ Does this person share my values, ethics, and goals for the business? This is very important! You must not hesitate to bring up these issues in initial discussions with your potential partner. If your partner's idea of business is to get rich quick at the expense of others, you might want to reconsider. Discuss with the potential partner both your short and long term business goals and determine if they mesh with his or hers. Better you find out about possible incompatibilities before making any formal commitments.

Ted and Bill were perfect partners, or so it seemed. Different areas of expertise, common goals, both had money to invest in the partnership. Because they were such long-time friends, they never talked with each other about issues that might cause problems in the future. They knew they had a good idea and worked well together and that seemed enough. Unknown to Ted, Bill was about to get a divorce. As female readers know, many men generally do not talk about personal matters, even among good friends, to any degree. Because of Bill's divided attentions, the partnership dissolved. Too bad, since altering the timing a bit might have saved the partnership and another good idea.

☐ If the partner is a spouse, does he or she share my same convictions about starting and operating a business? Refer to Chapter 8 for more information on home and business interactions.

☐ Does the potential partner share my qualities as an entrepreneur?

☐ Does this person have family or other personal problems? Be frank and ask the question! You are going to have enough problems with the new business and you cannot afford the additional stress that is brought on by non-business problems as well.

☐ How well do you know your potential partner? Like a marriage, you are going to be working together through good and bad times. Don't be too quick to get involved with someone who is just a casual acquaintance. Has this person been in a partnership before? How did it go?

Do not be quick to make a decision. An ineffective partner is much worse than no partner at all. When you have picked a partner, the next step is to formally (with the help of an attorney) lay out respective responsibilities of each partner. Plan to the extent possible, for unforeseen circumstances.

PARTNERSHIP AGREEMENTS

TRUISM 9

A well thought out and formally-executed partnership agreement is a must for a successful long-lasting partnership.

Formulate and execute your agreement early in the relationship before any possible problems come up. A partnership agreement should include, but not necessarily be limited to, the following items:

- Provisions for continuing the partnership in the event of death or withdrawal of one or more of the partners.

- Clear, easily understood "buy/sell" provisions in the event one partner wants to sell his interest.

- The partners' initial contributions and how profit/loss will be divided.

- Provisions that spell out the timing of withdrawal of partnership profits.

- Details of the partners' initial salaries and benefits.

- Each partners' responsibilities in the business.

In the case of two partners where the partnership being considered is a 50-50 split, some thought should be given to a 49-49-2 split with the 2% going to an outside individual who is mutually trusted by the partners and who would cast the deciding vote in any decision that cannot be agreed on by the partners. A stalemate can occur with a 50-50 split in which the partners simply cannot agree.

In any case, the partnership agreement should be reviewed by an attorney. In all likelihood, each partner will use his own attorney for this review.

SUMMARY

A well-chosen partner can increase your chances for success. Your partner can be a "sounding board" for ideas, a mutual problem solver, someone to share the work load, and bring added expertise (and capital) to your venture. However, choose your partner wisely and for the right reasons. When contemplating a good friend as a partner, remember Plato's words, "You can discover more about a person in an hour of play than in a year of conversation." In other words, ensure you really know your friend. And finally, remember to draw up and agree to a partnership agreement before any business is conducted.

CHAPTER 6
PLANNING FOR SUCCESS
(& FAILURE!)

"ED, I THINK WE NEED A PLAN WITH A LITTLE MORE SUBSTANCE."

WHY PLAN?

TRUISM 10

Planning is mandatory for business success. Fail to plan and you plan to fail.

In some ways this is the most important chapter in the book since planning is the single most important element in starting and operating a business. Amazingly enough, it is also the most overlooked. Lack of planning is the cause for the majority of business failures. If you only take one thought from this book, remember this:

> **START PLANNING FROM DAY ONE AND KEEP PLANNING THROUGHOUT THE LIFE OF YOUR BUSINESS. MODIFY YOUR PLAN AS YOUR BUSINESS GROWS AND AS EVENTS DICTATE.**

Planning is difficult because there is no immediate feedback as to its value. But if you think of starting and operating your business in the same way you might think about climbing the mountain that was mentioned at the beginning of Chapter 1, the purpose and advantages of planning become clearer.

When you start up the mountain you never know what to expect: sudden change in weather, lost or broken equipment, mistakes in maps, an injury. If you plan for these events, you will be able to deal with them and still reach top of the mountain in spite of the setbacks.

On the other hand, if you fail to plan, you will not be prepared to meet problems that happen due to circumstances beyond your control. This can be disastrous. If you take the time to plan carefully, you will anticipate more of the potential problems, find solutions, and be able to achieve your ultimate objective.

THE "BUSINESS PLAN"

Many books have been written on how to write an "effective" business plan and most provide good advice. The traditional business plan is a very well defined and structured document. You write it so that it can be shown to lenders, potential investors, and bankers in order to raise capital for the business. So, it's sort of an advertising document and, well, maybe tends to exaggerate a little.

Many people will argue that the business plan is a planning document. However, it frequently is not because of these exaggerations. After a while YOU will start to believe the business plan ... even if you know that what is contained within the document is absurd in places. (Yes sir, there is no doubt about it, sales will easily double each year ... as long as we can obtain adequate financing.)

If your business is going to require investor capital at the onset, you will need that traditional business plan. See the references listed at the end of this chapter for some examples of where to find information on preparing a traditional business plan. But BEFORE you even get to this point, or if you are like so many of us and are starting a small business venture where little or no formal investment is needed, you need another plan ... A plan for YOURSELF ... A HONEST plan for you. You need a strategic plan.

THE STRATEGIC PLAN

A strategic plan is your plan for success. It will define your business mission, your present situation, and where you want to be in three to five years. A strategic plan, like the traditional business plan, should be well-structured, and include a number of short succinct statements covering the following areas:

- Vision Statement
- Mission/Purpose Statement

- Scope of Business
- Assumptions
- Goals and Objectives
- Risks
- Strategies
- Progress Reporting Methods

Every statement in your strategic plan will be important since it defines what your business will be, what your objectives are, and how you intend to achieve these objectives. If you find you cannot write about the areas that are about to be discussed, you need to stop and think carefully about your situation until you can. A strategic plan will allow you to <u>anticipate problems</u> and to <u>make decisions</u> that will help you meet your business goals and objectives. Without a clear goal in mind, the best decision may not be obvious and you are reduced to guessing.

VISION.

This is a short statement that defines your overall long term goal. This statement should define WHAT your business will be. It should be brief (20-30 words) and clearly describe what you will be providing; and who the customer base will be. If the statement is too specific, it's not much of a vision; too general and it's unattainable. Your vision should be something to strive for ... usually a multi-year effort.

Poor:

"Provide the best automobile repair service in town." (too general)

"Build the largest Porsche repair garage in the country." (too general)

"Provide automobile painting services."
(poorly defined)

"Provide rebuilding services for 12-cylinder Ferrari engines." (too specific)

Better:

> VISION: Build an automobile repair business, specializing in Porsche, that will gain a reputation for outstanding service within the community and will, first and foremost, always be responsive to customers needs.

MISSION/PURPOSE.

This is a definitive comment that tells WHY you are pursuing your vision. Why do you want to start a business? What do you have to give? Keep in mind that a lot of people have a vision but very few have a mission ... At least one they are willing to pursue (many people shared Martin Luther King's dream but he was the one who also had a mission to do something about it). Think about what your mission really is.

> MISSION: Make use of my background and experience with Porsche automobiles to provide high quality repair and restoration services; to provide jobs for locally qualified individuals; to provide for my family's needs.

SCOPE.

You need to spell out the boundaries of your business. You cannot be everything to every-body. If the scope of your business is too narrow, the probability for success may be diminished due to the smaller number of potential customers. On the other hand, if the scope is too broad, you will never be able to achieve your objectives. You may make a few customers happy in the short term, but it is not a good idea to spread your energies over too broad an area.

Poor:

"Provide automobile repair service." (too broad)

"Provide Porsche repair services." (still to broad)

"Provide high performance engine modifications for Porsche." (too narrow)

Better:

SCOPE: We will provide our services for all Porsche automobiles with the exception of the 914 series. Our services will include general repairs and maintenance (less major body work), detailing, storage, rebuilding and restoring.

ASSUMPTIONS.

It is important to understand what specific assumptions you are operating under concerning your new business since they can determine and dictate how your business will grow and prosper. The more specific these assumptions are, the better. It may require a little research on your part to lay out these assumptions but the planning stage is the time to do it. It is difficult to give general examples, but in keeping with our Porsche repair facility, here are a few:

ASSUMPTIONS:

1. I will keep my present job for the next 12-months.

2. There are many Porsche owners in this area.

3. Present Porsche repair facilities are not perceived as doing a good job or being responsive to customer's needs.

4. My spouse will continue his/her current employment.

5. I will limit my involvement to 20 hours per week for the first 12-months.

6. I have fifteen customers that I can start with right now whose cars require major repairs.

GOALS & OBJECTIVES.

This is a listing of specific goals and objectives you want to achieve with your business. Think through this carefully. Your list should include items that can be "measured." This way you will know when you've achieved success. Goals should be realistic and doable within a one to three year timeframe.

Poor:

"I want to be independently wealthy."

"I want to be my own boss."

"I hate my job, I want to do something new and exciting."

"I want to be able to set my own work hours."

Better:

GOALS & OBJECTIVES:

1. Be able to quit my present job within 12 months.

2. Generate at least $150K gross sales in the first year of operation.

3. Add at least 100 new customers by the end of the first year of business.

4. Sponsor a racing team by the third year of business.

RISKS.

Identify as many risks as you can. This might be difficult since it requires some negative thinking, but it is important for you to consider the downside in your planning. A new business venture can be risky, but what is important is that you identify as many specific risks to your proposed business as possible. By doing this, you can plan to deal with the risks. In our example, consider the following:

RISKS:

1. Possible damage or loss of tools, inventory, facility.

2. Loss of customers due to the competition.

3. Loss of employee(s).

4. Loss of an important supplier.

5. Increase in cost of tools, parts, etc.

6. Loss of lease requiring a new location and facility.

Missing from the listing are "acts of God." Risks of this type are usually covered by insurance. Refer to Chapter 10, Protect Thyself.

STRATEGIES.

Once the risks have been identified, you can list the ways to deal with them. Your strategies are the methods you will use to achieve your goals and objectives in spite of the risks. Here are some proposed strategies for dealing with the above risks.

STRATEGIES:

1. Sponsor a monthly "clinic" in which we will provide the use of my facility to members of the local Porsche club. (generates loyal customers)

2. Provide parts at a discount and free advice for those taking advantage of the clinic. (gain a competitive edge)

3. Publish a monthly newsletter for all my customers. (excellent marketing)

4. Use direct mail to identify potential new customers and send them our newsletter. (keep looking for new customers)

5. Develop two reliable parts suppliers. (guard against loss of one)

6. Constantly reassess pricing with respect to the competition and costs.

7. Stay in close touch with my Realtor in terms of other locations in the event I have to move due to growth or problems with my current facility.

8. Be an employer worth working for ... treat my employees like the important asset they are. (See Chapter 11, Hiring and Working with Employees.)

PROGRESS REPORTING.

You will need to identify a way for periodically reporting the progress of the elements of your plan. If you write your plan and then forget about it, it doesn't serve the purpose for which it is intended. Your business is constantly changing ... many situations that affect your business are changing constantly and your plan must be updated or modified to reflect these changes. You must continually measure your performance against the plan. It is amazing how many planning documents are generated with great care and then placed in a drawer never to be looked at again. Don't you do it!

TRUISM 11

A plan that is not periodically reviewed and updated is nearly worthless

---

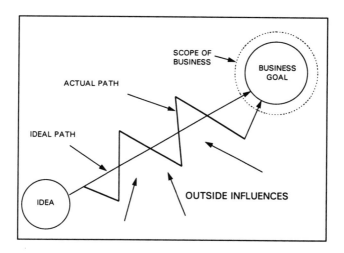

Figure 1

Figure 1 illustrates theoretical (ideal) and actual "paths" to reaching your business goal. The ideal path is a straight line directly from your idea to your goal. Unfortunately, theory can be far from practice and the actual path shown depicts more accurately what your trip will be like. As you move towards your goal, the influence of outside events will constantly force your direction to vary from the direction of the goal. You must update your planning to accommodate these influences and redirect your efforts in order to get back on the path to your goal.

The illustration also shows why you cannot change your goals in midstream. All previous planning is directed towards the current goal and moving the goal could negate all or most of your previous efforts since you are no longer pointed towards that goal! The illustration also shows why you must constantly readdress your plan ... Every time some external influence causes your progress to diverge from the goal you must immediately adjust your planning in order to get back on track.

Notice also the "scope of business" dotted outline surrounding the goal. What you see here is the importance of limiting the scope of business ... If it is too large your planning efforts may not home in on the goal (i.e., it will be difficult to "point" your path in the right direction).

Revisit your strategic plan monthly and revise and update it as required.

FAILURE

Your planning, if you have considered risks and especially the unexpected, should help you improve your chances for success. However, some businesses will fail for any of a variety of reasons. We've already talked about the fact that you must constantly update your plan to make sure it is tracking with changes as they happen. If you find, by referring to your planning documents, that you are not making satisfactory progress towards your goals, in spite of your best efforts, you must be ready to admit failure. Pull up stakes and cut your potential losses. Hanging on and watching your business slowly die can be financially and emotionally devastating. Alternatively, you might consider setting a new goal for a new business. In this case, the planning process starts again.

Perform a post-mortem and assess the failure. What went wrong? Were the circumstances beyond or within your control? Could the event(s) contributing to the failure have been anticipated and possibly mitigated?

In the true entrepreneurial spirit, you will probably be involved in a new business venture sooner or later and you want to be able to take advantage of your previous experiences. By spending time performing a careful assessment of your failure, you can document the lessons learned for future reference.

Lastly, you should be aware of this very important "planning for failure" truism:

TRUISM 12
Pay yourself first or you may end up with nothing for your efforts.

Do not make the mistake of putting every dollar of profit back into your business. Your business may very well prosper for a number of years and then be plunged into sudden bankruptcy through no fault of your own. If this happens, and, if you have not planned ahead, you may very well have nothing to show for your time or efforts. Plan for this disaster by remembering that YOU are the business and deserve to be appropriately paid for your efforts. Never forget to pay yourself first. In bad times, the creditors may hound you, but they will wait.

How much should you pay yourself? There is no easy answer or magic formula and it is difficult to give specific advice but some general guidelines are worth noting.

- If your business is equity financed, your salary should be formally determined based on a formula agreed to by the equity lenders. For example, the initial salary could be based on current monthly needs with subsequent in- creases as the business becomes profitable.

- If your business is debt financed (by yourself or others), your business or strategic plan should include your own salary and its basis. Clearly, if you are using your own money to finance a new business you probably won't initially take a salary. In this case you should ensure that your savings and any other sources of income will support you until you become profitable. However, as soon as the business starts re- turning a profit, start paying yourself a reason- able salary.

- Strike a balance between growth considerations and your salary. This will be different for each business but thoughtful planning will allow you to determine an effective split.

We all plan for success but in the world of small business, failure is all too possible, and for reasons beyond your control. So plan for both success and failure—don't return every dollar to the business— keep some for #1, yourself!

In terms of protection, you should be placing a certain percentage of your income into a retirement account such as a SEP or 401K plan. Money in these types of accounts is protected from creditors.

Plan ahead, you won't be sorry!

SUMMARY

Fail to plan and you plan to fail. This statement, or something similar, has been made in just about every business book ever written ... and many entrepreneurs still don't take it seriously! Be the exception ... plan, assess, and plan some more. You MUST have a clear goal and a well-defined methodology for getting there. Take all the time necessary to produce a well thought out strategic plan. Plan for your success but also plan for failure. Do this in part, by paying yourself first and having an appropriate savings program.

REFERENCES

ITEM	"The Business Planning Guide" by David Bangs, Jr
DESCRIPTION	Guide for preparing an effective business and financing plan
WHERE TO OBTAIN	Upstart Publishing Co., 12 Portland Street, Dover, NH 03820 (800) 235 8866
COST	$18.95 plus $3.50 shipping

ITEM	"The Business Plan: Your Roadmap to Success"
DESCRIPTION	Small Business Administration (SBA) videotape which teaches to essentials of developing a business plan.
WHERE TO OBTAIN	SBA Publications, P.O. Box 30, Denver, CO 80201; (202) 205 6665
COST	$30.00 plus $1.00 shipping
COMMENTS	Includes workbook

ITEM	SBA Publications associated with planning
DESCRIPTION	MP4: Business Plan For Small Manufacturers MP5: Business Plan For Small Construction Firms MP6: Planning And Goal Setting For Small Business MP9: Business Plan For Retailers MP11: Business Plan For Small Service Firms MP15: The Business Plan For Home-Based Business MP21: Developing A Strategic Business Plan
WHERE TO OBTAIN	SBA Publications P.O. Box 30, Denver, CO 80201-0030 (202) 205 6665
COST	$0.50 or $1.00 each plus $1.00 shipping/handling
COMMENTS	SCORE (Service Corps of Retired Executives) is an SBA affiliate association with offices in most major cities. Refer to local telephone book.

CHAPTER 7
GET PROFESSIONAL ADVICE

"WOULD YOU CARRY A LAWYER-CLIENT/CLIENT-LAWYER
DICTIONARY?"

W e've already mentioned a number of times that it's necessary to confer with your attorney and accountant (or certified public accountant, CPA). This chapter will give some basic advice on finding and dealing effectively with attorneys and accountants, as well as insurance agents, all of whom you should be contacting for advice on a regular basis. Another important professional is your banker who is discussed separately in Chapter 8.

It is very important that you seek advice often and early enough to keep you out of trouble. It's equally important that you are able to ask the right questions. One of the primary objectives of this book is to give you enough information so you are comfortable asking questions. You need to find business professionals with whom you are comfortable and have confidence. This is not always easy to do. Going to the Yellow Pages is probably not the answer. A better approach is to first ask for referrals from other small business owners. In this manner you can obtain a listing of individuals who are providing services in the areas of interest to you and you can begin a process of selection by interviewing.

TRUISM 13

Lack of professional advice often and early will surely cause problems sooner or later.

SELECTING AN ATTORNEY

This book frequently recommends that the advice of an attorney be obtained on various matters. You should be dealing with your attorney often and on a wide range of issues, so thoughtful selection is a must. Do not use attorney referral services, including the bar association in your area, since these services are generally "name brokers." What you need is a referral by someone who knows that a certain attorney is well versed AND INTERESTED in the problems of small businesses. A good place to start is with recommendations from your banker, accountant, and other owners of small businesses.

Meet with and interview at least three attorneys. Remember, you will be working closely with whoever you select and it can be difficult and expensive to switch later. During the interview you should try to determine if the attorney has an understanding of the problems associated with your type of small business and is interested in working with you. In all likelihood, you and your business will at best represent only a small percentage of the attorney's time so don't expect a lot of attention after the interview! You should also make certain you understand the rates and how you will be charged for services. Also, determine before the interview if you will be charged for the interview time. If you are not completely comfortable during the interview, move along to your next choice. Remember that you may get better service from one of the smaller law firms.

WORKING WITH YOUR ATTORNEY

Remember that attorneys are trained to solve problems and may not necessarily understand the business ramifications. They are, of necessity, generally very conservative. As such they may not have your entrepreneurial qualities. Keep this in mind when asking for their advice.

Do not blindly follow your attorney's advice ... ask lots of questions so that you <u>fully understand the basis for the advice</u>. Ask for any documents to be prepared in "plain text" and not "legalese." If legal terminology is used, make certain you understand the meanings. After you fully understand the advice and any associated documents, you may decide against it for reasons of your own. Your attorney's job is to ensure you are aware of the risk involved in making or not making a certain decision.

During one of my early business ventures, I asked my attorney for assistance in developing a contract form to use with my potential clients. Well, I got my form ... all three single spaced pages of it with a total of around 30 items! My attorney had attempted to protect me from every possible contingency but in doing so, generated a document so onerous that no one would sign it, including my current customers. I should have given my attorney more direction ... he assumed, in keeping with his training, that I needed as much protection as possible. With no customers, I needed no protection!

TRUSIM 14

Your business attorney will not
be proactive.

Since you are probably a very small client, your attorney will probably not be thinking about you unless you bring a <u>specific issue</u> to his or her attention. In other words, <u>you</u> need to find the potential problems and not wait for your attorney to alert you.

CHECKLIST #5:
WORKING WITH YOUR ATTORNEY

☐ Ask questions until you fully understand the issues and the "legalese."

☐ Remember that your attorney will not be giving advice from your entrepreneurial perspective but rather from a conservative point of view. The advice you get may or may not be right for YOU.

☐ Never hesitate to get another opinion on a specific matter if you are not completely confident with your attorney's advice. There is a tendency to take everything one hears from an attorney at face value.

☐ Ask for a cost estimates for every matter before you take it up with your attorney. Ask how expenses may be held down.

☐ Never, never be less than totally honest with your attorney.

☐ Ensure extra charges such as copying and faxes are being charged without padding. (The ABA requires lawyers charge actual costs for these extras).

☐ Ask for detailed invoices including hours spent on each item and review carefully.

☐ Invite your attorney to your place of business at least every 6-months to show him or her what you are doing. The better your attorney understands your business, the more effective the advice.

SELECTING AN ACCOUNTANT

Again, select with great care. Your prospective accountant should be a member of the American Institute of Certified Public Accountants (AICPA). Contact them at (212) 575-6200. The National Society of Public Accountants produces several useful booklets such as "How Accountants Set Fees." Contact them at (703) 549-6400.

Your accountant (or CPA), will be involved in every phase of your business and, if you are dealing with someone who understands the problems of a small business, you can benefit greatly from his or her advice. Your accountant can help you in the following areas:

- Setting up your books
- Selecting of an accounting package
- Tax planning
- Money management
- Setting up retirement plans
- Generating various financial reports
- Incorporation advice
- Dealing with the IRS
- Help with deciding to buy or lease

The advice given for selecting an attorney also applies when selecting your accountant. Locate and interview at least three. Select someone who is sensitive to the problems of your small business. A good accountant is a very valuable resource for you but, as with an attorney, it is up to you to get and keep their attention.

A good source of referrals for an accountant is your banker and owners of other small businesses in your area. Look to businesses that are closely related to yours in terms of operation: Manufacturing, retail, etc.

It is preferable to work with an independent accountant or very small firm to take advantage of the fact that you will probably represent more than a name on an invoice and the service received will be more personalized (they can grow as you grow).

However, we would be remiss if we didn't mention the potential advantages of working with one of the "big 6" accounting firms (for you who need to know, these are Price Waterhouse, Arthur Andersen, Ernst & Young, KPMG-Peat Marwick, Coopers & Lybrand, and Deloitte & Touche). These big firms have every conceivable accounting service available and are usually perceived to be so reputable that, in some cases, having your business audited by one of these companies as part of the paperwork for a loan can make the difference in obtaining the loan. However, as a small business, you may have a difficult time getting the attention you require. Or, for that matter, being able to afford them!

WORKING WITH YOUR ACCOUNTANT

Accountants will make suggestions based on a very conservative point of view, just like your attorney, and it is up to you to accept or ignore the advice and make the final decision. You, the entrepreneur, may always be testing the limits of whatever you are involved with, whereas the accountant will usually be quoting "from the book" on any given issue.

Some accounting chores, such as bank deposits, check writing, posting to your ledger, etc., can be satisfactorily handled by a bookkeeper whose services will certainly be less than that of an accountant. However, an accountant should be involved with preparation of your financial statements and all taxes to ensure statements are prepared in accordance with accepted accounting principles and that you are in compliance with all tax submissions.

Consider having your business accountant also prepare your personal tax returns so they can help with your financial and estate planning.

Numerous Federal and State requirements imposed on businesses with employees (See Chapter 11) makes payroll a complicated issue. Neither you nor your accountant need to get involved in this thankless task. It would be a poor use of your time and too expensive to use your accountant. Fortunately, there are excellent payroll processing services in nearly every major city throughout the United States. These services are inexpensive, complete, and, if a mistake is made, they pay any penalties that may be imposed by government agencies. Their services include preparing and delivering the checks, preparing the payroll register, sending all funds to the state and IRS, as required, preparing and filing all quarterly and annual reports. Check your local yellow pages for a service near you.

Checklist #5 (Working with your attorney) is also applicable to your accountant.

CHOOSING AN INSURANCE AGENT

Chapter 10 includes a discussion of the various forms of insurance you may be involved with in your business. You might glance at this chapter now just to take note of the variety and complexities involved with business and personal insurance issues. This will give you a better understanding of the importance of your insurance agent's role.

Once again, you should shop around and interview a number of commercial agents until you find one that you are comfortable with who understands your needs as a small business owner.

TRUISM 15
An independent insurance agent is most likely to provide unbiased advice.

Ask for references from the agent and, if possible, talk to another client who has had to make a claim against one of the agent's companies. Determine how helpful they were and how quickly and easily the claim was settled. You can learn a lot about an insurance company in this manner.

The agent you select must be aware of the details of your business. The interview with the agent should be at your place of business so that he or she can gain a better understanding of exactly what your business involves. This is especially important if you have manufacturing facilities.

It is a good idea to select an agent who is a Chartered Property/Casualty Underwriter (CPCU) and a member of the Independent Insurance Agents of America (IIAA). See references at the end of the chapter for additional IIAA information.

CHECKLIST #6:
WORKING WITH YOUR AGENT

☐ Invite the agent to your place of business on a regular basis.

☐ Be sure to keep the agent up to date on any changes that would affect your insurance program such as new employees or equipment, change of location, etc.

☐ Periodically, about every 6-months or so, review your entire insurance program to be sure you are adequately protected but not over-insured.

☐ When purchasing a new item requiring insurance coverage, call your agent and get a binder. Follow up within a few days to make sure the binder has been attached to your policy.

SUMMARY

Working with professionals such as attorneys, accountants, and insurance agents will be a fact of your business life. You are responsible for selecting these individuals and ensuring they are aware of your specific concerns and problems. They work for you and your responsibility extends to ensuring that you are getting good value for your money. The professionals you deal with, in most cases, may not understand your motivations as an entrepreneur, but they can help to keep you out of legal hot water. Listen to and make certain you understand their advice ... then decide if you want to accept it based on a clear assessment of the risks.

REFERENCES

ITEM	Independent Insurance Agents of America (IIAA)
DESCRIPTION	Association that licenses independent insurance agents
ADDRESS/TELE	127 South Peyton Street, Alexandria, VA 22314 (703) 683 4422
COMMENTS	Will provide help with specific insurance questions

ITEM	Guide to Professional Services by Leonard Bisk
DESCRIPTION	Selecting and managing lawyers, accountants and bankers.
WHERE TO OBTAIN	Entrepreneur Magazine, P. O. Box 1625, Des Plaines, IL 60017-1625. (800) 421-2300
COST	$19.95

"Tis a lesson you should heed; Try, try, try again. If at first you don't succeed, Try try, try again.

... W. E. Hickman

CHAPTER 8
ESTABLISHING A BANKING RELATIONSHIP

"MR. JASON, YOU LOOK LIKE THE TYPE OF PERSON WE CAN WORK WITH."

A bank is more than a place to keep your checking account and the bank you choose for your business activities can play an important role in your success. Different banks can provide a variety of services some of which you will need immediately, some will be of no interest whatever, and some you may need in the future. Typical business services provided include:

Checking Accounts
Saving Accounts
Foreign Drafts
Notary Service
Wire Transfers

Financing
Cash Management Services
Letters of Credit
Certificates of Deposit
SEP/IRA Plans
Lines of Credit
Receivables Financing
SBA Loans
Federal Tax Deposits
Merchant Credit Card Management

Also, a bank can provide valuable assistance and advice on money matters as they relate to your business. It's your responsibility to choose a bank that's right for your own needs.

CHOOSING A BANK

Consider what your specific business needs will be and if the bank you have in mind can provide them. For example, if you are going to be doing business in other countries you should make sure the bank can handle international transfers and is familiar with letters of credit.

Consider banks within your own community if you are engaged in a "community oriented" type of business. For safety reasons, if your business takes in a lot of cash, choose a bank with a branch near your location. Visit a number of banks in your area. Don't simply rely on the bank you have been using for your personal banking needs. Since services and the rates charged vary widely among banks it is wise to shop carefully. Seek suggestions from other business owners and your other advisors.

Visit banks that are large enough to provide the services you will need but no larger than necessary. The smaller the bank, the more personal the service and the more likely you can deal with a more senior level official (preferably the President) of the bank. During your visit make sure you cover the points in the checklist at the end of this chapter.

Once you have made your selection, arrange for a visit by a bank representative to your place of business, even if it is your garage. Your business is your greatest advertisement. Impress your visitor(s) with your knowledge of and enthusiasm for the business, show them any equipment related to the operation, and discuss your plans. But don't talk too much. Listen to the banker to find out what he or she wants to know about you and your business. Sell to the bank!

Although a bank may be Federally insured (FDIC), you should do some additional investigation to ensure the bank is safe and healthy. The easiest way to do this is to use the services on one of the companies that professionally analyze banks by reviewing their financial data and producing periodic reports, usually updated each quarter. The table at the end of this section lists three such companies.

CHECKLIST #7: CHOOSING A BANK

☐ Is the bank in a convenient location?

☐ Does the banker understand your business?

☐ Does the bank have an SBA loan program?

☐ Is the bank small enough so that you can deal with senior people?

☐ Is the bank a member of FDIC and the Federal Reserve Bank? (Commercial and savings banks are required to be a member of FDIC.)

☐ Does the bank provide the services you will need now and in the near future?

☐ Is the bank's capitalization/asset ratio greater than 6%? (This is a good measure of a banks "health") Calculate this ratio as follows: Divide the bank's "equity" (some-times referred to as "shareholders' equity" or "total equity") by "total assets" and convert to %. These figures can be found in the bank's financial statements, which the bank should gladly provide to you.

☐ What are the bank's fees for various trans-actions? Are they competitive?

☐ What are fees and interest associated with their credit cards? Are they competitive?

☐ What balances are required on interest-bearing checking accounts?

Company	Bauer Group, P.O. Drawer 14550, Coral Gables, FL. 33114-5510 (305) 441 2062
Product	Detailed 6-page analysis of 1 bank: $35 Detailed report of all banks in your state: $75
Company	Veribanc, Inc. Wakefield, MA 1 (800) 44BANKS
Product	Instant rating over telephone of 1 bank: $10. Short report on 1 bank: $25
Company	Sheshunoff Info Services, Austin, TX 1 (800) 456-2340
Product	6-page report analysis of 1 bank: $25 Detailed report of all banks in your state: $50

DEALING WITH YOUR BANK

Your bank is a service provider and as such knows that customer relations are important. However, if you are difficult to deal with, the service you receive may be less than satisfactory. When discussing any matter with your bank, always be pleasant and never demanding! If you can maintain a "gentle" approach even in the face of problems, you are more likely to get the help and advice you need and maybe even a little extra consideration.

Make yourself known at the bank.

TRUISM 16

The better your bank knows you, the more exceptional the service you will receive.

Visit from time to time so people know your face. Use these visits to keep senior-level bank personnel up to date on your business activities ... both good and bad. It may also be a good idea to provide the bank with your most recently revised business plan. The more the bank understands about what you are doing and your situation, the more they can help. NEVER, never hide information from the bank.

Stay up to date by reading the bank's annual report and attend the annual stockholders meeting. If possible, socialize with your banker. The banker with whom you occasionally dine or play tennis is more likely to be sympathetic to your business problems.

BANK LOANS

Your bank can be a prime source of business loans. When dealing with the bank for a loan remember that about 90% of their decision to loan is based on two numbers; your cash flow and current net worth. The remaining 10% of the decision is based on such items as credit history and continued business viability.

When approaching the bank for a loan make certain you have complete and up-do-date information concerning the present financial situation of your business. This would include, at a minimum, your business plan, personal balance sheet, business pro forma, and cash flow projections. The process will be much quicker and more likely to be successful with this information in hand. It can also be a very good idea to bring along your accountant ... they can talk the bankers' language perhaps better than you can.

TRUISM 17

Banks lending to a small business will generally require a personal guarantee from the owner.

Make the decision to give a personal guarantee only after you fully understand all the ramifications. You are now personally liable for the total value of the loan, if the business can-not pay. It does not make any difference if the business is incorporated, a partnership, or a sole proprietorship.

Banks frequently place liens against your personal residence as part of these guarantees and this can be done without your knowledge.

Personal guarantees are a fact of life for the small business person, so be prepared for them. Make certain you understand the worst case scenario.

Ted had been in the manufacturing business for about 3-years and was doing quite well. During this time he borrowed a number of times from his bank to purchase raw materials and some capital equipment. Without warning his major customer canceled their order (Ted's largest) and the business was left with considerable material which had been purchased for this job. Eventually Ted was forced into bankruptcy, first Chapter 11 and then Chapter 7. Ted had forgotten that he had personally guaranteed the loans when times were good and now was faced with having to deal with the bank outside the bankruptcy proceedings. Business or no business, Ted was solely responsible for the loans.

SUMMARY

Choose your bank intelligently and get to know your banker. He is a great source of information, can help you network within the local business community, and, possibly even more importantly, he may be your financial partner, holding the key to your business and personal financial survival.

Commerce is the great civilizer. We exchange ideas when we exchange fabrics.

... Robert Green Ingersoll

CHAPTER 9
SEPARATE HOME AND BUSINESS

"CAN'T WE TALK ABOUT SOMETHING ELSE AT DINNER TIME, BESIDES WORK?"

Lord Chesterfield (1773-1894) said, "Few people do business well who do nothing else." This is very good advice!

TRUISM 18

Effective and successful entrepreneurs do not become consumed by the business.

If your ONLY activity is your business, it is likely your family and social life will suffer. We all know people who are divorced today because of problems resulting directly from the pressures of starting and operating a business. Don't let this happen to you. This chapter will provide some guidance to help you keep some separation between your home and social life and your business enterprise.

What the quotation above tells us is that you are likely to lose some of the very qualities that will make you a business success if you don't remain well rounded in other aspects of your life. It should be clear to you by now that you will be spending a lot of time with your business but it is imperative that you also set aside time for family, friends, and yourself. Without this relief you are likely to burn-out long before you attain the success you want.

You will need the support of your friends and family and you may not get that support if you alienate everyone by not being sociable or not making time for them. By your very entre-preneurial nature, you are driven to be a success. But if you're not careful, and by your actions you lose those individuals who give real meaning to your life, you'll find your business success very hollow indeed!

TRUISM 19

Stay focused on your objectives but also strive
to stay balanced lest you lose
friends and family.

Here are a few specific suggestions for ensuring a successful marriage between your business and home life. You will probably be able to add to this list but the items included are those that have worked for others.

- Plan for the future but live in the present. Don't let the good times pass you by.

- Maintain a separate work area in your home for business activities. Use that area ONLY for business related activities.

- Keep your hobby(s) alive. Your hobby can be an excellent source of relaxation.

- Maintain some sort of physical activity. Working out is a wonderful way to reduce tension and clear your mind. (Don't forget to check with your doctor if you have not been active in the last few years.)

- Even if you have a home-based business, maintain separate personal and business bank accounts.

- When socializing, refrain from talking about business-related topics unless asked by others.

- Keep your spouse informed about your business activities but don't make it the only topic of discussion.

- Although you will be putting in long hours with your business, set aside regular time for family activities. (If you fail to do this you may not keep your family!)

The Institute for Family Business, Baylor University, was established to provide a forum for the development and dissemination of information to aid the continuity and health of the thousands of family owned businesses. A free newsletter is available. Contact the Institute by mail at P.O. Box 98011, Waco, TX, 98011, by telephone at (817) 755-2265, or by FAX at (817) 755-2271.

SUMMARY

Remember that problems with family and friends can spell disaster for your business. Be sensitive to their needs as well as your own. Stay involved in activities other than your business to the extent possible.

REFERENCES

ITEM	Tradeoffs (Executive Family and Organizational Life) by Greiff and Munter
DESCRIPTION	Published by New American Library. Good discussion about setting priorities to maintain a balance between "home" and "business" life.
WHERE TO OBTAIN	Bookstores, Library

ITEM	Honey, I Want to Start My Own Business by Azriela Jaffe
DESCRIPTION	A planning guide for couples. This book is required reading for every couple in business.
WHERE TO OBTAIN	Bookstores, Library

CHAPTER 10
MARKET! MARKET! MARKET!

"WE'VE GOT TO INCREASE SALES, EVEN IF IT MEANS CHARGING A FAIR PRICE."

Marketing takes in a wide area of activities but, in short, marketing is simply creating a demand for your product or services. Don't confuse marketing with selling, which is getting someone to actually purchase your product or service. Business success is much more dependent on marketing than on the product or service you are selling! As an entrepreneur you must be marketing (and ideally, selling) to every person with whom you make contact. Every dollar of services or products you sell will be the result of marketing. Knowing this, it is amazing how it can be forgotten. And once forgotten, it is frequently too late to recover.

TRUISM 20

Without marketing, failure is guaranteed.

You need to become familiar with basic marketing concepts and the purpose of this chapter is to introduce you to these basics. It won't make you an expert. There are literally thousands of references on the subject including books, tapes, and seminars. An excellent source of free marketing assistance is your local SCORE chapter. See references at the end of this chapter.

This chapter will specifically cover four major marketing steps:

1. Identification of target market
2. Pricing
3. Promotion
4. Distribution.

We'll also discuss keeping your customers (customer satisfaction) after your marketing efforts have found them.

Like so many entrepreneurs my first business started with a single customer. I was contacted, while employed in a regular job, by a company that wanted to purchase a few hours of my time in order to solve a problem they were having. I did so, made a few dollars, and immediately got a taste for the independence associated with working on my own. Eventually, as my association with this company grew, I quit my job and started an electronic manufacturing business supporting this one customer. My business grew to support their needs. Suddenly, due to a corporate realignment, my friend, the president was replaced. Unfortunately, one of the new president's associates was in the same business as I. You know the rest of the story. I lost my only customer! I was so busy supporting my "best" customer and monitoring my growth, I forgot that I might need other customers! I had not spent any time marketing! It was a foolhardy mistake.

Marketing essentially consists of these four major steps:

1. Identify product or service and potential market.
2. Determine the price.
3. Develop promotion strategies.
4. Assess distribution channels.

IDENTIFY PRODUCT AND POTENTIAL MARKET

Your planning activities should have included precise descriptions of your product and/or service along with potential markets. Your initial marketing activity will be to research these potential markets and make sure you chose correctly.

This research can take many forms such as direct mailing or personal interviewing. Even if you feel certain of your market segment, it is important to accumulate data based on more than intuition and observation. If you do not feel qualified to take on this research yourself you can hire a marketing firm. **If you go this route, make certain you understand what you will receive for your**

money. Marketing is more an art than a science (as most marketing individuals are quick to point out) and it is sometimes hard to define their product. It is also important that you have realistic expectations from whatever marketing methods you use. For example, direct mail response is considered good if you receive 1-2% reply. If you are expecting 50%, you and your marketing consultant are having some communication difficulties.

DETERMINE THE PRICE

In a way, this is part of your market research since you can collect information relating to what a customer might pay. You need to look at pricing from two aspects. On the one hand, what does it cost for the product (to manufacture, acquire, etc.) including your overhead and profit. On the other hand, what is the customer willing to pay for the product. Hopefully, these numbers will be such that you can reconcile a fair price for both yourself and the customer.

You obviously need to be competitive and that's where research is important. You must understand your competitors' pricing and ensure that you are either competitive or are providing a product or service that is superior in such a way as to command a higher price. What you can't do is take a head-in-the-sand approach and assign a price for your product or service that is not based on solid market research. For the most part, since you are already familiar with the territory, you will probably be able to perform this research better than a marketing firm. You'll also save some money in the process.

To help in determining the price of your product or service keep the following in mind:

- Your total cost.
- Your competitors' cost.
- What the market is willing to pay.
- What type of promotions you will use.

I hired a marketing consultant, to market my product development services. He wanted to market heavily in Florida for various reasons, including his contacts in the area, as well as that state's growth of companies that might need my services. We signed a contract that guaranteed him a monthly retainer for a year and defined his "services" in return for this retainer. He indicated that opportunities were vast in Florida and I could expect significant contracts as the result of his efforts. When the net results of his efforts were zero after 6-months, I was concerned enough to terminate his efforts in spite of the contract. We went to court and he prevailed. Our contract didn't state that his efforts had to result in any contracts. He got a year's worth of work from my company and I learned two things: 1) Write contracts very explicitly and have them reviewed by an attorney. Make sure you understand what you are getting for your money. 2) Marketing is indeed an art and specific guarantees are generally not possible. Also, the results of any marketing effort may take some time to become evident.

DEVELOP PROMOTION STRATEGIES

The possibilities for promotion are as varied as your imagination. See the following checklist for some ideas.

CHECKLIST #8: PROMOTION STRATEGIES

☐ Advertising on TV and radio

☐ Advertising in trade journals

☐ Advertising in magazines

☐ Advertising in newspapers/newsletters

☐ Personal contacts with potential customers

☐ Promotions (sales, open houses, etc.)

☐ Yellow Pages advertising

☐ Signs/displays

☐ Billboards

☐ Direct mail (see below)

☐ Seminars

☐ Your own newsletter

☐ Press releases

☐ Attendance at trade shows

☐ Publication of articles in trade journals, etc.

☐ Advertising/marketing on the Internet
  (See Chapter 14)

These are just a few examples. Your specific product or service and circumstances, such as location, will determine what works best for you.

DIRECT MAIL

Direct mailing campaigns, if used correctly, can be a very productive and cost effective promotion strategy. The uniqueness of direct mail is that you can target, through mailing lists, very specific groups of people. For example, those whose income exceeds some amount, those who own homes, a specific brand of car, or appliance, or who vacation in the Caribbean. The point being, you can get your sales message to the people most likely to take advantage of your offer. To properly take advantage of a direct mail program, you probably will need some help from someone in the business. However, knowing some of the basics of the direct mail business can be an advantage.

- As with all aspects of marketing, you need a well-defined plan with a budget.

- Timing of mailings is important. Statistics show that January, February and October are the best, June and July the worst.

- Prepare your mailing piece thoughtfully ... you get only one chance. It's a good idea to get professional assistance here. A good copywriter can be invaluable. Once again, shop around and ask lots of questions. Make sure you know what you are buying.

- Choose mailing lists carefully. List costs vary but an average is $50 per thousand names for one-time use. Don't try to cheat and use the list more than once ... owners normally "seed" the list and you will be found out.

- Keep detailed records of returns (unde-liverable mail) you receive. Reviewing this data will allow you to more effectively select future lists.

- If you will purchase labels from the list provider, determine if your labels will be manually or machine affixed. You need to order the labels in the correct form.

- When you receive returns from your list mailing, you may now use those names to generate your own mailing list.

- Make certain you understand the following specifics of the list you purchase:

    1. The total number of names.
    2. How the list was compiled and its date.
    3. List profile (how the list was complied.)
    4. The media on which the names will be provided (labels, computer disk, etc.)

- Consider using a full-service mailing house who will take care of all the details for you. As always, shop around and ask questions.

- Test the list before purchasing a large quantity of names. Purchase 1000 to 5000 names and analyze the returns.

- Have realistic expectations. Responses from list mailings are very low.

ASSESS DISTRIBUTION CHANNELS

Distribution channels are the methodology of getting your product or service to the customer. The items of interest here include:

- Location of your business (most important for retail operations).

- Using wholesalers and distribution centers.

- Packaging and shipping details.

The specifics of your product or service will determine what else may be important. What's critical is to consider distribution in your overall planning efforts.

* * * * *

Depending upon the particular circumstances of your business it may make sense to use a marketing firm to set up an integrated marketing program. Remember, however, that when dealing with the marketing firm you, and only you, are responsible for what you get out of the relationship. Shop before selecting and make sure you understand what to expect from the service.

GET THE WORD OUT

Marketing is also promotion. Here are a few ideas for promoting yourself and your business.

- <u>Write an article</u>. Think about it. You're an expert in something so tell the world. Write an article for one or more of the magazines in your area of expertise. Many will pay you for the article but even if they don't it's worth the effort since your article byline can gain you publicity. [My bylines always include a mention of one of my books and how to order a copy!]

- <u>Present a Seminar</u>. If you have the expertise and background, this is a great way to present your information to a number of people simultaneously and get paid for it. Also, a seminar is a great way to sell your product such as a book, report, etc. An excellent reference on how to develop and promote a seminar is "Successful Seminars & Workshops" by Howard Shenson which is available in many bookstores.

- <u>Produce an Audiotape</u>. (or CD) A cassette audio tape or CD is inexpensive to produce and duplicate. Audio tapes relating to self-help topics are great sellers. Check your yellow pages or better yet, the Internet for sources of cassette and CD producers.

- <u>Install a FAX-on-DEMAND System</u>. This allows a customer to call your number and request specific documents be fax'ed back to them. The system is fully automatic and is like having an additional employee who works 24 hours a day responding to customer requests for infor- mation. A number of companies provide fax-on- demand systems. Check out Faxback on the Internet at http://www.faxback.com or call them at (800) 329 2225.

- <u>Produce a Videotape</u>. If you're presenting semi- nars or other sessions have them videotaped. These tapes can be packaged and sold for more than the cost of the original seminar! Video production companies in your area can be found in the yellow pages.

- <u>Give a Speech</u>. Make yourself available as a speaker in your area of expertise. Even if you don't get paid for the presentation, the exposure is worth your time. A good way to begin is to make yourself known to your local library association who frequently are looking for pre- senters on a variety of topics.

- <u>Generate Information</u>. Regardless of what you do or sell, create an informational report or brochure about the product or service. Produce it to read like a learning tool and include useful information for the reader. Be sure to include ordering details for your product or service. Advertise your report via e-mail, direct mail, and in your other business literature. Sell it for enough to cover your production and mailing costs. You will generate a mailing list at no cost to you AND sell your product or service. Printing companies such as "Sir Speedy" can produce these packages quickly and very inexpensively.

CUSTOMER SATISFACTION
(Keeping your customers)

Your marketing program exposes your product or service to potential customers. Hopefully the program will also bring these customers to your door. Once at the door, the trick is to keep them. It's really simple to do this ... keep your customers satisfied. The old adage is true, "Your best advertisement is a satisfied customer." A customer satisfaction program is a must for your business. Also remember that it is less expensive to retain an existing customer than to find a few one.

Put yourself in the place of the customer when assessing your performance. It is frequently the little things that make a difference. The following checklist highlights a few tried and true elements of a customer satisfaction program. Please take note that some of these suggestions apply only to certain types of businesses.

CHECKLIST #9:
CUSTOMER SATISFACTION PROGRAM

☐ Make sure that ALL your employees understand that the customers are #1.

☐ Never, never argue with a customer.

☐ Treat EVERYONE as a potential customer.

☐ Don't use a telephone answering machine or a voice mail system unless absolutely necessary. Customers like to talk to real people, not machines. Think how irritating it is for you to wade through the typical voice-mail "menu." But, choose a machine over an answering service. With a machine you know what will be said to the caller.

☐ Answer the telephone by the second ring.

☐ Say "Thank you" frequently ... be courteous.

☐ Provide something free (coffee, bagels, pens).

☐ ALWAYS return telephone calls promptly.

☐ Answer your own telephone.

☐ Handle all complaints quickly and personally if required.

☐ Install a complaint "hot line" for customers to use.

☐ Make your product/service easy to purchase.

☐ Arrange for purchase by credit card.

☐ Have an "open house" periodically.

☐ Provide free samples.

☐ Sponsor a free lecture.

☐ Don't oversell (don't be a pest but be there when needed).

☐ Call your own office from time to time just to see how you're treated.

☐ Go the "extra mile" for your customer.

☐ Don't ever blame anything on a "computer problem."

☐ Have a sale just for "preferred" customers.

☐ If you deal in an expensive product or service with few customers, follow up each sale with a telephone call or written communication.

☐ Use customer satisfaction surveys. You will always learn something that is surprising.

☐ Stay visible within your community (volunteer your time, join toastmasters).

Thinking about how you would like to be treated is your best guideline. Be sure to periodically review your customer satisfaction program and make changes, if needed.

TRUISM 21

You never know who your next customer will be, so treat <u>everyone</u> as a potential customer.

SELLING TO THE GOVERNMENT

There is one unique customer we should briefly discuss before leaving the subject of marketing — The United States Government, who just happens to be the world's largest consumer of goods and services. It is a mistake to think that just because you are a small or new business that this giant customer is out of your reach. In fact, <u>most</u> purchases by the government are from small businesses! Appendix VIII includes specific information for marketing to the government.

SUMMARY

<u>Market every day</u> and treat every person you meet or talk to as a potential customer. Remember that your largest or oldest customer can disappear tomorrow and whatever marketing techniques you use will need time for results.

REFERENCES

ITEM	"United States Government-New Customer!" by Robert Sullivan
DESCRIPTION	A step by step guide for selling your product or service to Uncle Sam. (540 pages)
WHERE TO OBTAIN	Information International P. O. Box 579, Great Falls, VA 22066. (800) 375 8439
COST	$27.95 plus $5.00 shipping/handling

ITEM	"Street Smart Marketing" by Jeff Slutsky
DESCRIPTION	Published by Wiley & Sons. Discusses creating and implementing a sales plan and techniques for boosting sales.
WHERE TO OBTAIN	Bookstores, Library

ITEM	Service Corps of Retired Executives (SCORE)
DESCRIPTION	A program of the Small Business Administration (SBA) which matches retired volunteers with small businesses that need expert advice in specific business areas.
WHERE TO OBTAIN	National SCORE® Office 409 3rd Street, SW Suite 5900, Washington, DC 20041-3212 (202) 205-6762
COST	Free

ITEM	"Creating Customers" by David Bangs, et.al.
DESCRIPTION	Step by step approach for selling and promoting. Market research techniques, pricing, writing a marketing plan, etc.
WHERE TO OBTAIN	Upstart Publishing Co., 12 Portland Street, Dover, NH 03820 (800) 235 8866
COST	$19.95 plus $3.50 shipping/handling

ITEM	"The Complete Selling System" by Pete Frye
DESCRIPTION	Sales techniques
WHERE TO OBTAIN	Upstart Publishing Co., 12 Portland Street, Dover, NH 03820 (800) 235 8866
COST	$21.95 plus $3.50 shipping/handling

ITEM	"How to Win Customers & Keep Them for Life" by Michael LeBoeuf
DESCRIPTION	A good reference text.
WHERE TO OBTAIN	Bookstores, Library
COMMENTS	Also available on cassette from Nightengale-Conant Corp., (800) 323 5552

ITEM	"Marketing Your Products and Services Successfully" by Harriet Stephenson and Dorothy Otterson
DESCRIPTION	Detailed descriptions of marketing concepts.
WHERE TO OBTAIN	PSI Research, 300 North Valley Drive, Grants Pass, OR 97526 (800) 228 2275
COST	$18.95

ITEM	"Direct Mail Magic" by Charles Mallory
DESCRIPTION	A practical guide for effective direct mail advertising. Includes postal regulation information.
WHERE TO OBTAIN	Crisp Publications, Inc. 95 First Street, Los Altos, CA 94022 (800) 442 7477
COST	$8.95

ITEM	"Marketing without Megabucks" by Shel Horowitz
DESCRIPTION	How to sell anything on a small budget. Lots of great and practical information.
WHERE TO OBTAIN	AWM, P. O. Box 1164, Northampton, MA 01061-1164 or call (800) 683 9673
COST	$15.00 ppd

ITEM	Various SBA Publications
DESCRIPTION	MT1: Creative Selling ... The Competitive Edge MT2: Marketing For Small Business ... An Overview MT3: Is The Independent Sales Agent For You? MT4: Marketing Checklist for Small Retailers MT8: Researching Your Market MT9: Selling By Mail Order MT10: Market Overseas With U.S. Government Help MT11: Advertising
WHERE TO OBTAIN	SBA Publications, P. O. Box 30, Denver, CO 80201-0030 (202) 205 6665
COST	$0.50 OR $1.00 each plus $1.00 shipping/handling
COMMENTS	SCORE (Service Corps of Retired Executives) is an SBA affiliate association with offices in most major cities. Refer to your local telephone book.

Do not delay, the golden moments fly!

...Henry Wadsworth Longfellow

CHAPTER 11
PROTECT THYSELF

"OKAY, FERGUSON, WE HAVE A VERBAL AGREEMENT—
BUT I'D LIKE MY LAWYER TO CHECK IT OUT."

What do we mean by "protection?" Protection includes those steps we should take to ensure continuity of business operations in the event of unforeseen problems. It also includes protecting your personal assets from business creditors in the event of a business problem.

Part of owning and operating a business includes being fully aware of the potential liabilities that may result from any number of situations, such as selling a product to someone who is subsequently injured by it; being sued by a customer or business associate; or damage to your facility. The list is endless and the watchword is "awareness." Once aware of the potential problems, you can take steps to limit your liability and business disruption in the event of an unforeseen circumstance. Keep in mind that as a practical matter, you can only limit your liability, not reduce it to zero. You must take steps to keep your potential liability at acceptable limits. That is, how much can you afford to lose without becoming "insurance poor" (buying too much insurance).

Protection includes the following major elements:

- Choosing the most suitable business legal structure.
- Obtaining legal advice when required.
- Fully understanding personal guarantees.
- Using credit bureaus.
- Developing an insurance program.

BUSINESS LEGAL STRUCTURE

The various business legal structures are explained in Chapter 3. They range from the sole proprietorship to various forms of the corporation. As we said earlier, it is difficult to give specific advice as to what is best for you. Take the time necessary to understand the various advantages and disadvantages of each business legal structure. The legal structure you choose relates directly to your potential personal liability and, therefore, to your insurance program. Always consider your personal exposure when selecting your legal structure.

LEGAL ADVICE

We discussed the need for legal advice in Chapter 6. What needs to be stressed again at this point, is that protection starts with appropriate legal advice on any and all contractual matters relating to your business. Review Chapter 6.

Don't take any chances. In the legal world, after the fact is nearly always too late. With legal matters, don't be penny wise and pound foolish! Business legal problems can sneak up on you and you must be ready. You get ready by having your attorney review contracts and other business documents before signing them. DON'T be pressured by time constraints or the excitement of the moment!

TRUISM 22

A personal guarantee is never a problem at the time you sign it.

Don's business was going well. He had an opportunity for a large purchase order with a company many times his size. The order was straightforward, indicating a delivery date for manufactured items at a stated unit cost. Don was excited ... the order was the largest he had ever received and, in his haste, he immediately acknowledged the purchase order and set to work. Unfortunately he had not reviewed the BACK of the purchase order which listed "conditions of sale" in about this size type. Don's major supplier was tardy with materials which, in turn, made his delivery late. The customer refused to accept delivery! The "fine print" made it clear that late deliveries would not be accepted. Too bad.

PERSONAL GUARANTEES

The best advice here is think twice and then think again! With a personal guarantee, you are liable for the guaranteed amount regardless of your business legal structure. Personal guarantees are usually executed when business is going well so one tends not to think of the downside.

Do not EVER sign a personal guarantee on the spot. Have the guarantee reviewed by your attorney ... these documents can be onerous. Review the guarantee considering the worst case scenario. It may be difficult to think worst case when all is going well but you must assess from this perspective.

Kathy signed a personal guarantee for a commercial lease to be used by her incorporated business. The leasing company required the guarantee because the business did not have adequate assets. No big deal, Kathy thought. It was a 5-year lease and the guarantee only covered the first year at the full yearly lease value. Thereafter it decreased to a fraction of this value. Her business was expanding and she needed the space now. All was going well. One year later disaster struck and the corporation went into bankruptcy. Kathy was now personally responsible for the remainder of the lease AND (as noted in the fine print in the lease) the cost to rebuild the space for the next leaseholder.

With personal guarantees (and indeed, anything you are considering signing), recall the advice of H. Jackson Brown, Jr., in his "Life's Little Instruction Book" in which he notes, "Read carefully anything that requires your signature. Remember the big print giveth and the small print taketh away."

CREDIT BUREAUS

It might seem strange to consider protection from your customers but the fact is, while your customers are one of your greatest assets, they are also your biggest potential problem makers. Good relationships can turn bad overnight. If your customers are other businesses, they can have problems, too.

When you contract with a customer you need to maximize your chances of getting paid for your efforts. Since most businesses are not cash-based, you will be forced to provide credit terms to be competitive. You should always ask for credit references. However, rest assured that your potential customer will not knowingly give you a "bad" reference. You need an independent check and that's what credit bureaus can do for you. For a very minimal charge or no cost, you can check your customers' credit rating from an independent source. The major credit bureaus are listed at the end of this chapter.

If your customer is a corporation, consider using Dunn and Bradstreet (D & B) services for checking past payment history and related information.

If your business will be incorporated and you will be dealing with vendors, consider obtaining a credit rating from D & B for your own business. See the reference section for additional information.

TRUISM 23

A customer whose credit you check will always be a good risk ... don't check and it will be bad.

Check credit of EVERY customer before accepting his order. If you have any doubt about the possibility of being paid, request payment prior to shipment or performance of your services. Don't be shy about this. If you are questioned, simply indicate that your check of their credit was not satisfactory.

INSURANCE

The importance of insurance cannot be over-emphasized and neither can the danger of paying for insurance you don't need. We will briefly discuss the various types of insurance that you should consider for your business and also strongly recommended you solicit the advice of an independent business insurance agent. Don't forget to SHOP! Talk to three or four independent agents and compare notes and prices. An insurance agent will lay out a vast array of insurance coverage much of which you simply may not need. Your situation will be unique and you must consider each insurance element carefully to ensure comprehensive coverage.

In some cases, insurance coverage can be obtained at favorable group rates through various professional associations such as the Chamber of Commerce. Check with your own professional associations.

Whatever your final insurance program looks like, you should review it at least every six months. Your business can change rapidly, especially in the first few years and insurance needs change with it. Keep your program up to date by calling in your agent and reviewing your coverage. Make changes where necessary.

Liability Insurance. This is probably the most important element of your insurance program. Liability insurance provides protection from potential losses resulting from injury or damage to others or their property. Just recall some of the big cash awards you have read about that have resulted from law suits concerning liability of one kind or another and you will understand the importance of this insurance. Your insurance agent can describe the various types of liability insurance coverage that are available. If you will end up with a comprehensive general policy, make certain that the general policy does not include items you don't need. Pay for only the insurance you need. For example, your business may not need product liability insurance.

Do not confuse business liability coverage with your personal liability coverage, both of which you need. Your personal coverage will not cover a business-generated liability. Check to be certain.

Compare the costs of different levels of coverage. In some cases a $2 million policy costs only slightly more than a $1 million policy. This economy of scale is true with most forms of insurance coverage. That is, after a certain value, additional insurance becomes very economical.

> ESI was a small firm run by three partners, a software programmer, marketer, and a general manager. Their product was a complex computer program used by aerospace firms. Ed, the programmer, was involved in a severe automobile accident, became totally disabled, and ESI lost their programming capability. The problem was that the computer program written by Ed was essentially the company's sole product. Modifications to accommodate the customer became impossible and the time to bring another programmer up to speed was excessive. ESI lost considerable business as a result of this situation. These losses could have been offset by key person insurance.

Key Person Insurance. This type of insurance is particularly important for the sole proprietorship or partnership where the loss of one person through illness, accident, or death may render the business inoperative or severely limit its operations. This insurance, although not inexpensive, can provide protection for this situation. Key person insurance might also be necessary for others involved in your business.

Disability Insurance. You, as a business owner, should be covered by disability insurance whether or not you decide on key person insurance. This insurance, along with business-interruption insurance, described below, will help ensure your business will continue to operate in the unfortunate situation where you are unable to work. Your disability insurance policy needs to provide satisfactory coverage. Particular attention should be paid to the definition of "disability," delay time until payments start, when coverage terminates, and adjustments for inflation.

Fire Insurance. Fire insurance, like all insurance is complicated and you should understand what IS and IS NOT covered. For example, a typical fire insurance policy covers the loss of contents but does not cover your losses from the fact that you may be out of business for 2-months while your facility is rebuilt. Fire insurance is mandatory whether you're working out of a home office or you have a separate facility. You should discuss a comprehensive policy with your agent. Take the time to understand the details. For example, will the contents be insured for their replacement value or for actual value at the time of loss?

Consider a co-insurance clause which will reduce the policy cost considerably. This means that the insurance carrier will require you to carry insurance equal to some percentage of the value of your property. (Usually around 85%.) With this type of clause it is very important that you review coverage frequently so you always meet the minimum percentage required. If this minimum is not met, a loss will not be paid no matter what its value.

If you are working out of your home, your existing homeowners policy may not cover business property. If this is the case, have your insurance agent to add a home-office rider to your policy.

Automobile Insurance. You probably already have automobile insurance but it might not include business use of your vehicle. Make sure that it does.

Worker's Compensation Insurance. If you make the decision to hire employees, you will be required, in most states, to cover them under worker's compensation. The cost of this insurance varies widely and depends on the kind of work being performed and your accident history. It is important that you properly classify your employees to secure the lowest insurance rates. Work closely with your insurance agent.

Business Interruption Insurance. This protects against loss of revenue as the result of property damage. This insurance would be used, for instance, if you could not operate your business during the time repairs were being made as a result of a fire or in the event of the loss of a key supplier. The coverage can pay for salaries, taxes, and lost profits.

Credit Insurance. This will pay for unusual losses as the result of nonpayment of accounts receivables above a certain threshold. As with all policies, you must thoroughly understand the details so discuss it with your insurance agent. One of the largest providers of this coverage is American Credit Indemnity, Baltimore, MD. (800) 879 1224.

Burglary/Robbery/Theft Insurance. Comprehensive policies are available that protect against loss from these perils, including by your own employees. Make certain you understand what is excluded from coverage.

Rent Insurance. This policy covers the cost of rent for other facilities in the event your property becomes damaged to the extent that operations cannot continue in your normal location.

Disability Insurance. This insurance will pay you an amount each month slightly less than your current salary in the event you become disabled and are unable to work. Cost for this coverage varies considerably depending on your profession, salary level, how quickly benefits start, and when they end. Benefits paid are tax-free only if you, not your company, pay the premiums.

This list could be continued since it is possible to purchase insurance for just about any peril you can imagine ... if you can pay the premium! When considering your insurance coverage, use the following checklist:

CHECKLIST #10: INSURANCE COVERAGE

☐ Can you afford the loss?

☐ What coverage is required by Federal, state, or local law?

☐ What SPECIFIC items are covered by the policy?

☐ Are items to be insured for their replacement cost or original value?

☐ What SPECIFIC items are EXCLUDED by the policy?

☐ If there is a co-insurance clause, do you have adequate coverage?

☐ Have you chosen deductibles wisely in order to minimize costs?

☐ Do any of the policies you are considering duplicate or overlap one another?

☐ Do you need any insurance based on location, e.g., flood, earthquake?

Use the following checklist to review your insurance plans:

CHECKLIST #11: INSURANCE PLAN

☐ Employ an independent insurance agent rather than going to individual insurance companies. Ensure the agent shops for your insurance.

☐ Talk to and get quotations from at least THREE agents and pick the best one for you.

☐ Use money saving comprehensive policies, if possible.

☐ Perform periodic (every 6-months) reviews of your insurance program.

☐ Have business assets professionally appraised to determine coverage needs.

☐ Ensure existing personal insurance coverage includes business-related activities and add riders as necessary or obtain additional coverage.

SUMMARY

Protecting your personal assets is a vital part of your business planning. It is important to consider possible liabilities before disaster strikes. Select an insurance agent who can lay out a comprehensive, cost-effective insurance program. Use legal services when required, check on your customers credit in a timely fashion and be careful with personal guarantees. Make certain you understand your insurance policies.

REFERENCES

ITEM	SBA Small Business Risk Management Guide MP 28
DESCRIPTION	This guide provides assistance in identifying and minimizing business risks and specifically discusses insurance programs and guidelines to help you deal with an insurance professional.
WHERE TO OBTAIN	U.S. Small Business Publications P.O. Box 1000 Fort Worth, TX 76119. (800) 827-5722 Most SCORE offices can provide copies of SBA guides.
COST	$1.00
COMMENTS	SCORE (Service Corps of Retired Executives) is an SBA affiliate association with offices in most major cities. Refer to your local telephone book.

ITEM	Dunn and Bradstreet Services (D & B)
DESCRIPTION	Provides corporate credit information as well as other services.
WHERE TO OBTAIN	Call your local D & B offices or 1 (800) 234 3867 for more information. You may also write to D & B Information Services, Customer Service Center, 8310 N. Capital of Texas Hwy, Suite 200, Austin, TX 78731

ITEM	"SBA Hotline Answer Book" by Gustav Berle
DESCRIPTION	This book is a summary of hundreds of the most asked questions of the U.S. Small Business Administration (SBA) along with comprehensive answers.
WHERE TO OBTAIN	Library or any book store.
COST	$14.95
COMMENTS	Worth the cost. Full of useful information and easy to read.

ITEM	Credit Rating
DESCRIPTION	Provides information about your own credit rating or the credit rating of current and potential clients.
WHERE TO OBTAIN	Equifax 1600 Peachtree St., NW Atlanta, GA 30309 (404) 885-8000
COST	Call for fee information.

ITEM	Credit Rating
DESCRIPTION	Provides information about your own credit rating or the credit rating of current and potential clients.
WHERE TO OBTAIN	CSC Credit Services 652 Northbelt, Suite 133 Houston, TX 77060 (713) 878-4840
COST	Call for fee information.

ITEM	Credit Rating
DESCRIPTION	Provides information about your own credit rating or the credit rating of current and potential clients.
WHERE TO OBTAIN	Trans Union Credit Information Co. 555 W. Adams Blvd. Chicago, IL 60661 (312) 258-1717
COST	Call for fee information.

ITEM	"Business Continuation Planning"
DESCRIPTION	SBA Publication MP20. Life insurance needs of a small business.
WHERE TO OBTAIN	SBA Publications P.O. Box 30, Denver, CO 80201-0030 (202) 205 6665
COST	$1.00 plus $1.00 shipping/handling

ITEM	"Personalized Financial Planning Guide for Self-Employed Professionals & Small Business Owners" by J. D. Pond
DESCRIPTION	Excellent information on business and personal insurance coverage as well as other financial topics of interest to the entrepreneur.
WHERE TO OBTAIN	Bookstores or library
COST	$6.95

Being good in business is the most fascinating kind of art ... Making money is art and working is art and good business is the best art.

... Andy Warhol

CHAPTER 12
HIRING AND WORKING WITH EMPLOYEES

"WE'RE LOOKING FOR IMPARTIAL PEOPLE WHO THINK THE WAY WE DO."

Employees ... who need's 'em? Depending on your specific business, hiring employees may be necessary, but the responsibility of having employees is awesome. This chapter deals with the complexities of this responsibility. Hiring, employee policies, specific employer responsibilities, working with employees on a daily basis, and alternatives to hiring employees is covered.

"REAL" COST OF AN EMPLOYEE

Add to the employee's wages the cost of benefits expected by most employees (including health insurance which is getting more expensive daily!), the cost of your additional tax and insurance liabilities plus administrative time, and suddenly your $20,000 per year secretary is costing you $50,000! Hiring the employee is the easy part (and even that process can cause you problems). With even just one employee, you are now required by law to be aware of and implement a sea of regulations. This is both expensive and time consuming and with your hands full starting and running your business you should think twice about this additional responsibility. In the event you determine employees are mandatory (we'll talk more about this later), hiring is the first hurdle.

TRUISM 24

The "real" cost of an employee is approximately 2½ times his or her yearly wages.

HIRING

Potential problems with employees start with the hiring process. You can get yourself into trouble by simply asking the wrong questions during an interview. For example, you cannot ask applicants for any of the following information:

    Age or birthplace
    Ethnic origin or nationality
    Race or Religion
    Marital status or number of children
    Disabilities
    Arrests

There are numerous state and Federal anti-discrimination regulations that you must not violate. With only a few employees, you are exempt from some of these regulations, but not all. A discussion of these regulations is beyond the scope of this text; however, an excellent way to become familiar with the most recent applicable regulations is to attend one of the many hiring (and firing) seminars that are available from time to time in most major cities. Watch the business section of your newspaper for seminars in your area and use the references at the end of this chapter for additional sources.

A common method for finding employees is to run advertisements in your local newspaper or journals. Be careful! You must word your advertisement so that one class of individuals is neither specifically included nor excluded. Prior to placing an advertisement, pass the copy by your attorney for review ... just in case.

The above advice also applies to your employee application form ... there is much information you cannot ask for such as social security number, gender, race, labor union membership, marital status, height, weight, and more. Have your attorney review it!

Your application form should, however, ask for references, and you should check them all. Although a former employer, by law, can't reveal too much about a former employee, there is one question you can ask requiring a "yes" or "no" answer that is the most important information the former employer can give you, "Would you hire this person again?" You should also verify the information the applicant gave you such as employment dates and salary.

TRUISM 25
You get what you pay for.

If and when you do decide to hire, hire the best.

Hire individuals who are smarter than you are in what they do. The reason you hire employees is to extend your expertise or perform tasks you cannot perform yourself. Take your time and do not settle for second best. Every person who works for you will be representing YOU and your company. Think about that before you say, "You're hired."

EMPLOYEE POLICIES

An employee policy manual is mandatory. It must be comprehensive since it will set forth all the policies you and your employees will live by relating to the employee-employer relationship. This policy manual should include items such as ...

Working hours
Vacation, sick leave, leave of absence
Holidays
Benefits
Compensation
Pay periods, overtime pay
Salary review periods
Time off policy
Training
Retirement
Grievances
Promotion
Performance reviews

Termination
Substance abuse
Dress policy
Smoking

Many samples of employee policy manuals are available. Don't try to write your own from scratch ... you're sure to overlook something and besides, you're reinventing the wheel. Get an example and modify it to suit your needs then have it reviewed by your attorney.

Changing your policies can be painful so try to get it right the first time. The references at the end of this chapter suggest some additional sources on the subject.

EMPLOYER RESPONSIBILITIES

Your responsibilities will grow as your number of employees grows but the list is long even with one employee! This section is limited to those items of interest for companies with less than 100 employees ... that should hold you for a year or two! Unless otherwise noted below, you are responsible for the item even if you have a just one employee. The following list is not exhaustive but it does cover the major items. Your attorney and your accountant will be able to fill in the details where necessary. Do not take any of these items lightly since non-compliance can bring heavy fines and possibly law suits.

The paperwork nightmare includes ...

- Collecting and paying FICA taxes.

- Paying employer social security taxes.

- Paying Federal and state unemployment taxes.

- Maintaining worker's compensation insurance.

- Maintaining an employee benefit plan (this is not a formal requirement).

- Complying with Employee Retirement Income Security Act (ERISA). This is a very complex regulation and requires the assistance of your attorney and your accountant to ensure compliance in your specific case.

- Complying with Occupational Safety and Health Administration (OSHA) requirements.

- Complying with the Federal Fair Labor Standards Act (FLSA), including child labor, minimum wage, and overtime payment.

- Complying with Federal and state anti-discrimination laws. (Most of these laws are not applicable unless your business has fifteen or more employees.)

- Complying with immigration law requirements, as applicable.

Is this enough for you? There are probably more coming and you have be continually aware of developments in all these areas. That translates into legal and accounting fees in addition to the various taxes you are responsible for as an employer.

One last item to consider before hiring employees: In the unfortunate likelihood that you must declare business bankruptcy, payroll taxes, such as social security, are not discharged debt. You will be personally liable for these payments as well as the possible severe penalties.

UNEMPLOYMENT TAXES

As previously noted, you will be responsible for payment of Federal and, in most cases, state unemployment taxes. The rate you pay is a function of how many of your former employees claim and receive unemployment benefits and can range from .8% to more than 6% of the first $7,000 of annual wages per employee. Because of this, most businesses fight each claim that is presented against it. The law is complicated in this area and you must be very careful how employees leave your employ. Professional advice is mandatory from your accountant.

The following listing, excerpted from "Starting and Operating a Business in [state]," and reprinted with permission from The Oasis Press® and M. D. Jenkins, Copyright 1991, is a series of tips on how you can keep down the number of unemployment claims filed against your business.

- Be aware, when you are hiring, of the cost, if you have to lay people off. You may hire a number of new employees for an expansion or new project with the view that, if things don't work out as planned, you will simply lay them off and cancel the project with no further cost. Not so! Remember that if you do have to lay them off, you may be paying a much higher unemployment tax for several years as a result.

- Document in writing your reasons for firing an employee, if for reasons such as theft, insubordination, absence, or intoxication on the job. This will buttress your argument that the fired employee is not entitled to benefits if he or she should file a claim.

- Be aware that if you change an employee's hours of work and he or she quits as a result, it will be considered involuntary dismissal and the employee will probably be eligible for benefits. So it pays to have a written agreement signed by the employee to work any shift, hours, weekends, etc., that may be required. Then if the employee quits it will not be due to a change in job conditions, in the eyes of the law.

- If you decide to fire someone for cause, do it on the spot. If you keep them on at your convenience until you find a replacement, it will not usually be considered a discharge for misconduct, and the fired employee will most likely be eligible for benefits. It is a good idea to have someone with you when terminating an employee to protect yourself against possible future misinterpretations.

- If new employees do not work out, consider firing them before they have worked three months. In most states, a person has to work for you at least three months before they can earn unemployment benefits that are chargeable to your reserve account.

ALTERNATIVES TO HIRING EMPLOYEES

In almost all cases, the help you will need may be obtained by contracting for the services you require. These services may be in the form of temporary workers hired through an agency or by using another company for the work required. This arrangement will make your legal life much simpler but does not relieve you of the responsibility of selecting the best person (or company) for the job or making sure you are getting the most for your money.

When looking for help, it is generally possible to find the help you need either by contracting through an agency or directly with a person or company as an independent contractor. What you pay may seem high but remember what you are saving by not having a "regular employee." In cases where manufacturing is part of your business, consider subcontracting the various manufacturing processes to appropriate vendors.

> Joseph was doing quite well with his small manufacturing business but lamented the fact that he spent too much time with employee problems ... not an uncommon complaint. We reviewed his manufacturing costs and started looking for contract help. We located small companies to purchase and quality control materials; perform the manufacturing process; and finally to a company which provided the testing, packaging, and shipping. Joseph was able to reduce his staff to one ... himself. Cost of manufacture went up, overall costs decreased, and profits increased. An added benefit to Joseph was a lot more free time to pursue other business activities.

Joseph's solution is not an uncommon one but there is one caveat with this technique: Select reliable sub-contractors and provide for backups in case one fails you. It is up to you to make sure that quality assurance UP TO YOUR STANDARDS is being practiced by each company you deal with. Do not contract with anyone who cannot provide you with a satisfactory quality assurance manual.

Remember, you are responsible for your product.

Finding the help you need on a contract basis can be easier than you may think. Countless individuals are looking to "moonlight." An excellent place to look is at your local universities, colleges, and trade schools. In some cases, if you find the right person(s), you can always offer stock or other ownership in your company. Sometimes this kind of trade is well worth the expertise you can attract.

A word of caution about independent contractors. It is up to you to ensure an individual you hire as an independent contractor meets various "tests" for both legal and tax purposes. A mistake can make you liable for a number of different fines, back payroll taxes, legal damages in the event of injury, and others. The IRS looks very carefully at whether a worker is an employee or independent contractor, since you, the employer, avoid paying social security and unemployment taxes for independent contractors.

The most basic test for determining if an individual is an employee or independent contractor concerns how he or she is managed. Your worker is an employee if you decide what the job is and how it is to be accomplished. The worker is an independent contractor if he or she is given a job to do but with no further instructions as how to accomplish the task. Sometimes the distinction is easy to make, and other times not so obvious. Because of this, the IRS has a long list of audit guidelines to assist in making this determination. The details of these guidelines are beyond the scope of this book. Contact your accountant and ask to discuss the contents of IRS Audit Manual Exhibit 4640-1. The IRS also provides Form SS-8, which contains information for use in determining if a worker is an employee for purposes of Federal employment taxes and income tax withholding. See references at the end of the chapter for details on how to obtain this form.

LEASING EMPLOYEES

Another interesting alternative to hiring your own employees is to lease the employees you need through a leasing firm. You pay the leasing firm a small fee and the payroll costs and they, in turn, take care of all the legal headaches associated with employees such as compliance, claims, payroll, tax and insurance, as well as providing a benefits package. Make sure the leasing company you deal with is a member of the National Staff Leasing Association (NSLA). See the references at the end of the chapter for where to obtain additional information on this approach.

WORKING WITH EMPLOYEES

Dealing with employees (contracted or yours) is always challenging and will tax your best management and leadership skills. There are numerous books dealing with managing people and management techniques and you can spend a lot of time reading about this subject. However, there are two small books on the subject well worth acquiring: "The One Minute Manager" by Blanchard and Johnson and "Putting the One Minute Manager to Work" by Blanchard and Lorber. These two entertaining texts contain a lot of practical and wise advice for working with employees.

The following listing, based on a good deal of experience, are items to consider that will help keep you out of trouble when dealing with your employees:

CHECKLIST #12: WORKING WITH EMPLOYEES

☐ Be willing to pay for the best. Remember, you get exactly what you pay for ... no more and no less.

☐ Everyone has their own way of doing things. We all seem to forget this and insist it be done "our way." A better approach is to give instructions as to what is needed and allow the individual to provide the method.

☐ Remember to always criticize in private and to praise in public.

☐ Remember that EVERYONE needs to feel appreciated. Talk to your employees and make certain they know they are providing a valuable service.

☐ Stay visible. Make certain all your employees see you at least once a day. Your employees need to know you're involved and interested.

☐ Keep your promises. If you say you're going to do something, do it! There are no good excuses in the eyes of your employees.

☐ Ask your employees for suggestions on a regular basis. Do this personally ... not just with a "suggestion box."

☐ Allow your employees to fail! It is well documented that successes are generally preceded by one or more failures. The employee who is afraid to fail will be less likely to be innovative.

It is up to you to see that none of these failures is fatal to the business.

☐ Every employee must know exactly what their responsibilities are and what authority they have for carrying out these responsibilities. This usually is accomplished by very precisely written job descriptions.

☐ Manage by objectives. Each of your employees should be assigned (by mutual agreement) specific goals to be obtained within a certain period of time. These goals must be measurable and you will periodically review them so that corrective action, if needed, may be taken to get back on track. Managing by objectives stresses real results as opposed to a job description which only lists the individual's responsibilities. (The references at the end of this chapter give some more sources of information on this subject.)

☐ Constantly motivate your employees to do a good job. Talk to them about their job and its importance to the business. Maintain an "employee-of-the-month" program with an appropriate certificate and a traveling trophy. Make the monthly presentation with fanfare.

☐ Implement an effective training program to encourage promotion. Any employee who thinks they are in a dead-end job will not perform up to expectations.

☐ Remember the "Peter Principle"... to paraphrase: Everyone rises to their level of incompetence. See that this does not happen in your business.

SUMMARY

Think twice before making the decision to hire employees. The resulting expense, responsibilities, and complexities may not justify the convenience. Consider the alternative of leasing or using independent contractors. If you do hire employees make sure you hire the best and treat them accordingly. It's the least you can do, after all, your employees represent you and your business.

REFERENCES

ITEM	"The Personnel Planning Guide" by David Bangs, Jr.
DESCRIPTION	Recruiting, interviewing, hiring, and paying employees.
WHERE TO OBTAIN	Upstart Publishing Co., 12 Portland Street, Dover, NH 03820 (800) 235 8866
COST	$18.95 plus $3.50 S/H

ITEM	"The Peter Principle" by Peter and Hull
DESCRIPTION	A satirical but insightful look at how individuals move up in an organization
WHERE TO OBTAIN	Bookstores, library
COMMENTS	MUST READING !

ITEM	"Problem Employees" by Wylie and Grothe
DESCRIPTION	Approaches to dealing with problem employees.
WHERE TO OBTAIN	Upstart Publishing Co., 12 Portland Street, Dover, NH 03820 (800) 235 8866 FAX (603) 742 9121
COST	$22.95 plus $3.50 S/H

ITEM	"Hiring the Best" by Martin Yate
DESCRIPTION	Published by Bob Adams, Inc. An excellent reference with great interview ideas and questions for various positions.
WHERE TO OBTAIN	Bookstores or Library

ITEM	"Starting and Operating a Business in <state>"
DESCRIPTION	Covers current Federal and state laws that affect businesses. Many samples of government forms and where to obtain assistance. Includes sections on business legal forms, buying an existing business, starting a business, operating the business, and specific state laws. Separate book for each state.
WHERE TO OBTAIN	PSI Research, Inc., 300 North Valley Drive, Grants Pass, OR 97526 (800) 228 2275 FAX (503) 476 1479
COST	$21.95
COMMENTS	Highly recommended reference

ITEM	IRS Form SS-8, "Information For Use In Determining Whether A Worker Is An Employee For Federal Employment Taxes And Income Tax Withholding"
DESCRIPTION	IRS informational form that is useful is determining if a worker is an employee or independent contractor.
WHERE TO OBTAIN	IRS

ITEM	Various SBA Publications
DESCRIPTION	PM1: Checklist For Developing A Training Program PM2: Employees: How To Find And Pay Them PM3: Managing Employee Benefits
WHERE TO OBTAIN	SBA Publications P.O. Box 30, Denver, CO 80201-0030 (202) 205 6665 Most SCORE offices can provide copies of SBA guides.
COST	$0.50 or $1.00 plus $1.00 shipping/handling
COMMENTS	SCORE (Service Corps of Retired Executives) is an SBA affiliate association with offices in most major cities. Refer to your local telephone book.

ITEM	Hiring and Firing Seminar
DESCRIPTION	Covers numerous aspects of hiring and firing employees.
WHERE TO OBTAIN	Keye Productivity Center, Box 23192, Kansas City, MO 64141 Call for details, (800) 821 3919
COST	$125
COMMENTS	This full day seminar is presented regularly in major cities throughout the country. Keye also presents seminars on a wide variety of business topics including management practices, time management, selling, vendor/supplier relations, interviewing, etc. Call for additional information.

ITEM	"MBO II" by George Odiorne
DESCRIPTION	Published by Fearon Pitman Publishers, Inc. A full length reference on management by objectives.
WHERE TO OBTAIN	Bookstores, library

ITEM	National Staff Leasing Association
DESCRIPTION	This association can provide information on employee leasing as well as make referrals to leasing firms in your area.
WHERE TO OBTAIN	1735 North Lynn Street, Suite 950, Arlington, VA 22209-2022 (703) 524 3636

Nothing great was ever achieved without
enthusiasm.

... Ralph Waldo Emerson

CHAPTER 13
GET TECHNOLOGY SMART

"OPEN UP CLAYTON. YOU KNEW IT WAS INEVITABLE."

To be competitive in business, you must be able to utilize the technology that is available to assist you. This includes computers, FAX machines, and copiers. This chapter will describe in some detail, the selection, purchase, and utilization of a personal computer in your business activities in order to make you more efficient and more profitable. FAX machines and copiers will be briefly addressed. Lastly, the Internet is introduced along with suggestions for "getting connected."

INTRODUCTION TO COMPUTERS

Simply stated, a computer is a MUST for your business. A properly used small "personal computer," as they have become known, can be an incredible time saver. Examples of what you can accomplish with a personal computer include...

- Composing correspondence from simple letters to complex advertising brochures, including artwork and fancy print fonts.

- Analyzing and forecasting business data with easy to use "spread sheet" programs.

- Storing virtually any kind of information with the ability to quickly retrieve any specific item(s).

- Maintaining bookkeeping and tax records.

- Tracking accounts receivable and accounts payable.

- Payroll administration.

- Generating and maintaining mailing lists.

- Keeping track of customers and their preferences.

- Inventory control.

The list could be extended indefinitely since the software that is available for personal computer systems is amazing in its breadth and scope. Furthermore, even the most basic personal computer system is incredibly powerful.

If you are not "computer literate," an excellent way to gain a quick and inexpensive education is to attend an introductory computer course at your local community college. As a general rule, these college courses are better than those given by many local computer dealers, since you will not be subjected to a sales pitch for the brand of computer being sold by the dealer, which may or may not be the best for you. Also look through a few of the computer magazines available at all bookstores and newsstands. *PC World* and *PC Magazine* are two examples of monthly periodicals.

A computer cannot work magic. It is merely a tool that is only as good as the information you put into it. A computer is really a simple device and only operates and modifies data and information it has been given. It cannot correct your mistakes! There is a well known computer acronym to keep in mind; GIGO: "Garbage In, Garbage Out."

SELECTING A COMPUTER

There are two major (small) computer "platforms" in common use today:

1. The IBM® personal computer and its many "clones" (inexpensive versions of the IBM personal computer available through a number of manufacturers and compatible with IBM software and hardware). These computers use the DOS® and Windows operating system.

2. Apple personal computers (Macintosh®).

IBM and Apple users are very opinionated with respect to which platform is best. I'll simply state here that we prefer the IBM platform because of the vast amount and variety of software that is available and will say no more about the two systems except to note that the remainder of this chapter is written based on IBM platforms. Keep in mind that for the most part, software that runs on the IBM system will not run on the Apple system and vice versa. (Note: Some newer versions of the Apple will run both kinds of software.)

As suggested previously, purchase a few of the many computer periodicals available. Review the various advertisements and get a feel for what equipment is being advertised, the "packages" available, and costs. Reviewing these periodicals will also introduce you to the terminology used. The idea is not to become a computer expert, just an informed buyer.

You will need both "hardware," the computer equipment itself, and "software," the programs that make the computer useful to you by allowing it to perform specific tasks such as word processing. The following short glossary of computer terminology will be useful in helping you under-stand the material to follow.

GLOSSARY OF COMPUTER JARGON

Processor.
This is the brains of the system. These days, nearly all computers use some form of the Pentium microprocessor. It's speed, and hence the perform-ance of the computer, varies from 133 to over 200 Megahertz.

Older computer systems use microprocessors that operate from less than 33 to around 100 Megahertz. These use microprocessors designated by a number that defines their series and speed. For example a computer designated 386-40 is a 386 series microprocessor operating at 40 Megahertz. These older computers can be quite satisfactory for some simple applications such as word processing and are available for a few hundred dollars.

Memory.

This is the component in which the computer stores information. The two major types of memory are "volatile" and "non-volatile." Volatile memory loses its data when the computer's power is turned off whereas non-volatile memory will retain its data even after power is removed. The most common type of volatile memory is random access memory (RAM) and is associated with the processor itself. Non-volatile memory includes read-only-memory (ROM), which you cannot change, that provides the processor with basic instructions it needs to operate. The most important memory parameter is size. Size is measured in bytes of data and normally expressed in millions of bytes or megabytes or thousands of bytes or kilobytes.

Byte.

This is the basic unit of information used by the processor. Generally, since many bytes are required for information to be of use to us, larger units are utilized. For example, kilobytes (thousands), megabytes (millions), and gigabytes (thousands of millions). A short letter written using a word processor might be 3 kilobytes in size; the word processor software itself is a few megabytes in size; and a large database could be hundreds of megabytes.

Storage.

These are the computer's "file cabinets." There are a large variety of storage devices available and the most common are described in the table below:

TYPE	SPEED	SIZE	COMMENTS
3.5" disk	slow	1.44M	Most popular removable storage media today.
5.25" floppy	slow	360K, 1.2M	Common removable storage media (not used much any more).
Harddisk	fast	20M->5G	Internal storage necessary for running software efficiently.
CD-ROM	fast	>600M	Generally read only. Read/write CD-ROM devices are still quite expensive.
Harddisk, removable	fast	20M-500M	Type of media that can be removed from the computer. Good for keeping backups.

(K = kilobytes, M = megabytes, G = gigabytes)

Operating System.

This is the software that provides the background tasks required for your computer to run useful software. The most common systems in use today are Windows 3.11™ or Windows95™ In general, the operating system and interface will be furnished when you purchase the computer. If not, ask for it and have it installed before you buy. If you have a choice, ask for Windows95.

Monitor.

This is the video output device (screen) and is either monochrome or color with the most popular sizes being 15, 17 or 21 inches (measured diagonally across the screen like a television set). Virtually all monitors sold with computer systems are color with 15 inches the most popular size.

Video Card.

This plugs into the computer and "drives" the monitor. The card required depends on the monitor chosen and how which multimedia applications you will be using. You must have one for your system.

Keyboard.

The typewriter-like keyboard that you use to enter data into the computer. The most popular is the "101" key type which includes a separate "number grouping" and "arrow grouping," both of which are very handy.

Ports.

These comprise the hardware that allows you to connect external devices to your computer such as printers, mouse, scanners, etc. There are two types, serial and parallel. Serial ports are more flexible and parallel ports are faster. Serial ports may be used to connect a mouse or modem to the computer and most printers will require a parallel port. Virtually every computer sold today includes at least one of each type.

Mouse.

This popular pointing device is used to move the cursor around the monitor screen.

Modem.

The device allows your computer to be connected to another computer via a telephone line (connecting to a bulletin board or to the Internet for instance). It may be a small external box or be included inside the computer itself. (For example, you might transfer financial data to your accountant via a modem.)

Printer.
There are numerous varieties available with great variations in speed, accessories, appearance of output (black & white or color), etc. Common types includes the laser and inkjet. Prices range from $100 to the stratosphere.

* * * * *

SOFTWARE

The computer is of no value without software (programs). Everything the computer does requires specialized software. Fortunately, the amount of software that is available today nearly boggles the mind. There are literally thousands of programs from which to choose. However, you will need only a few of the following programs to get started:

- Word processor. This is the program that allows you to generate different types of correspondence from a simple memo to long complex documents. Current word processors are extremely powerful and are mandatory for business operations today. Your letters and other correspondence take on a professional look that is simply not attainable any other way. There are a number of word processors on the market. Features of most word processors include a variety of text formatting features (underlining, bold, italics, overstrike, etc.), deletion and insertion of characters, words, paragraphs, etc., search and replace capability, page numbering, automatic index and table of contents generation, headers/footers, and support for all popular printers, to name but a few.

> Suggestion: Microsoft Office 95 which includes Microsoft Word 7.0.

- Spreadsheet. The spreadsheet is probably responsible for the very existence of the personal computer. It is a program that allows you to produce a matrix of cells each containing text or numbers and for which you can perform a variety of calculations by "inserting" simple or complex formulas within each of the cells. The spreadsheet is a powerful tool, since every time you change the contents of one of the cells, all the other cells are automatically updated based on your formulas. In effect, you have a changeable "model." You can use spreadsheets for performing all types of financial analysis and keeping track of data. A spreadsheet truly puts the power of a large "mainframe" computer into your hands through your table top personal computer.

- Harddisk maintenance program. Your harddisk will require periodic maintenance (described below) and this is accomplished by very specialized software, which is included within the operating system and Windows™.

> Suggestion: Microsoft Windows 95 includes a harddisk defragmentator and general maintenance utility.

- Disk backup software. THIS IS MANDATORY SOFTWARE. You will need a program for "backing up" your data in the event you have a problem which destroys the data stored on your harddisk. The marketplace provides plenty of choices. See the section on computer security later in this chapter.

  Suggestion: Use a removable drive such as the 100Mbyte Omega ZIP drive for backups.

- Accounting package. This is the software that will track your accounts receivables and payables, maintain the general ledger (if required), provide inventory control functions, track capital equipment, generate business reports and more. It is indispensable! Prices for these packages have dropped from thousands of dollars to the $150 - $350 range.

  Suggestion: "Quick Books" by Intuit at a cost of less than $85. This software package is perfect for the small sole proprietorship. It is easy to use and its features include invoicing, check writing, report generation, transaction history displays, customer informat-ion lists, 1099 generation, accounts receivable and payable activities and more. It is well worth the price.

CAUTION: Select accounting software with the help of your accountant. It is highly desirable to purchase software already being used by or is familiar to your ac-countant.

- Utilities. Utilities are software programs that make your computing life easier. They are designed to save you time and frustration. Once familiar with their function, you will wonder how you got along without them. We will refrain from making specific suggestions (well, maybe a couple) but what follows is a list of a few of the utility programs that you will find to be useful or absolutely required:

Telephone dialer. These programs allow you to maintain a phone directory along with numbers and related information with search capability. With an appropriate modem you can dial a selected number automatically.

> Suggestion: Microsoft Windows 95 includes a basic telephone dialer.

Disk optimization. These programs, when run periodically, maximize the efficiency of your harddisk.

> Suggestion: Microsoft Windows 95 includes a maintenance utility.

Virus protection. A computer virus is some computer software (code) that gets into your system and can be a minor irritant or cause major damage to your system. The computer "catches" the virus from external software being loaded into the machine, usually by modem. A virus utility can look for a virus and then clean it out of your system. The virus utility should be run periodically. Cost of these utilities is less than $50 ... cheap protection.

> Suggestion: Consider McAfee VirusSan.

File recovery utility. These allow you to recover files that have been accidentally erased. The first time you need it, you will agree that this utility is worth its cost many times over.

Suggestion: Norton Utilities

The suggested software in the previous paragraphs may be purchased from any local computer store or mail order vendor. Always comparison shop since prices can vary widely.

So then, what do you really need ... at least to start? If you visit ten computer stores you will get ten opinions, if you ask ten friends with computers you will get ten more opinions. If you read on, you'll get yet another. The fact is, that with all the equipment and software that is available the possible combinations are nearly infinite! At the risk of getting into all kinds of trouble, we are going to recommend a starter system that should be adequate for your initial needs regardless of what your business will be.

At first, one system should be adequate for the task. Later, when your business grows, and more than one person needs the use of a computer, you can add systems as needed and "network" them together with readily available software and hardware.

The chart on the following page is my suggestion for a "starter" system. Your favorite computer expert will no doubt disagree with some items, but nevertheless, it's still a good place to start.

The CD-ROM player deserves special mention. More and more software is being supplied on CD-

ROM. Many computer systems include a CD player as part of their "standard" package.

SUGGESTED "STARTER" SYSTEM:

ITEM	COMMENTS
Desktop system with Pentium 166 processor	Should include at least 3 expansion slots for adding hardware accessories such as internal modem, additional ports, and multimedia accessories.
16-Mbyte RAM memory (more, if you can afford it)	Most systems include 16-Mbyte of memory as a standard feature. The more memory, the better.
512K cache memory	Normally included as a standard feature. A larger size cache will increase the speed of your system for some applications.
1 serial and 1 parallel port	Normally included.
CD-ROM player	At least 12X speed.
3.5" Floppy Drive	Mandatory
1 gigabyte harddisk (bigger is better)	Many systems are being supplied with 1.6 or 2.1 gigabyte harddisks
Color video card	Should include at least 1-Mbyte on-board memory.
Color monitor	Should be "non-interlaced" for flicker free operation. 15-inch minimum size.
101-key keyboard	Most convenient to use.
Mouse	Required for most software.
Windows for Workgroups, 3.11 or Windows95	Frequently included with the computer as a standard feature. If not, make sure this software is installed in your machine before delivery.
Service Agreement	If inexpensive, get one.

The approximate cost as this is being written (August, 1997), for our "starter" system is around $1300-$1500 through a number of reputable mail order firms. In addition to the hardware and software items in the chart, you will also need the software suggested previously and a printer to meet your needs. Printers are discussed later in this chapter.

As a specific example, for $1300 you could purchase a Micro Express PCI/166 which utilizes a 166Mhz Pentium and includes 16Mbyte of RAM, 512Kbyte cache, 2 gigabyte harddrive, CD-ROM player, and 15-inch color monitor.

PURCHASING YOUR COMPUTER

The most economical and efficient way to purchase your computer system is through one of the many reputable mail order firms presently engaged in the sale of IBM clone systems, software, and various peripherals. From time to time the more popular computer magazines (noted previously) contain reviews of the various mail order vendors. Review back issues at your local library.

Select a vendor that has at least a 30-day money back guarantee (many have 60-day return policies) and PAY BY CREDIT CARD. DO NOT SEND A CHECK TO ANY MAIL ORDER VENDOR. Payment by credit card gives you recourse in the event you have problems with the vendor. When ordering do not be hesitant to negotiate ... there is tremendous competition between the various mail order houses. If possible, purchase everything you need as a package since it puts you in a better position to negotiate. Observe the following when dealing with mail order computer suppliers.

Some popular and highly rated mail order manu-facturers include Dell, Gateway, and Micron. An example of a reputable mail order vendor that can supply a variety of systems, software, and acces-sories is CDW, (800) 631 4239.

CHECKLIST #13: PURCHASING BY MAIL

☐ Shop! Prices vary widely and there are many companies from which to choose.

☐ Do not be afraid to ask questions ... no one can see who you are!

☐ Get the name of your sales person.

☐ Does the price include shipping? If it does not, how much extra?

☐ Do you have to pay sales tax?

☐ Is everything in stock? When will goods be shipped?

☐ Make certain your credit card will not be billed until the equipment is actually shipped.

☐ Is there a restocking fee? How much? Who pays return shipping?

☐ What is the warranty? Money-back guarantee? For how long?

PURCHASING YOUR PRINTER

The printer is normally a separate item and not part of a basic system due to the variety of features and cost. Because of this, it is difficult to be very specific with advice but here is a short checklist when considering the purchase of your printer.

CHECKLIST #14: PURCHASING YOUR PRINTER

☐ What quality and speed do I need? Usually, the better the print quality, the slower the speed. By quality we mean what the output looks like and by speed we mean how fast can a page be printed. The best buy for the money, if high quality is not required, is a 24-pin dot matrix printer and there are numerous models from which to choose. They are quite fast, easy to use, and fairly inexpensive. If you need high quality (text that looks like what you are now reading) and if you will be working with graphics, you should consider an ink-jet or laser printer. By far the most popular are the laser models by Hewlett-Packard. Laser printers are considerably slower than the dot matrix units, but the output is simply beautiful. They can be more expensive, however.

> Caution: Often overlooked is the cost of owning the printer. A dot-matrix unit only requires a ribbon replacement periodically at a cost of $2.00 to $5.00, and a printer head maybe once in a lifetime at around $20.00. The laser requires a new "toner cartridge" every few thousand pages at a cost of around $60.00.

☐ What features are required? Printers are available with a variety of features including provisions for single sheet or continuous form paper feed, various fonts (appearance of the individual characters), ability to print graphics, ability to print in color, ability to feed more than one type of paper, printing envelopes, etc. When considering your selection, make sure you have considered what the use of the printer will be.

To assist you in your printer selection, here are a couple of examples with typical discount prices.

> Okidata ML390 24-pin dot-matrix, $340
> Epson LQ570 24-pin dot-matrix, $250
> H-P 694C color ink-jet printer, $300
> H-P 6P laserjet printer, $730

The major advantages of a dot-matrix printer are its cost, speed and the ability to utilize pin-feed paper and forms. The major advantage of a laser printer is its high quality output and the ability to print graphics.

COMPUTER OPERATIONS

You will probably use your computer daily for a variety of tasks and as time goes by you will come to rely upon the data that it contains as well you should. However, since the computers available these days are so reliable and easy to use, it is not difficult to forget that certain precautions need to be taken to ensure continued proper operation as well as assurance that your data will always be available to you. These precautions can be divided into three areas:

1. Regular maintenance,
2. Backing up data, and
3. Security.

REGULAR MAINTENANCE

The most obvious item of maintenance is simply keeping the computer clean. Wipe the monitor screen from time to time with a soft cloth (special cleaning pads are available from most computer supply stores); keep foreign material from falling into the keyboard and don't keep your coffee where an overturned cup will spill into the keyboard. From time to time, make sure the cooling fan exit grill (at the rear of the computer cabinet) is clear of any material that might block air flow.

A not so obvious maintenance item is the harddisk. If you remember that your harddisk contains all your data files and software, you might be more inclined to give it some loving care. This care can be accomplished with simple and inexpensive software that is designed to read the disk and repair damaged portions to ensure continued data integrity and maximum performance. One excellent example of this type of program is SpinRite-II available through software mail order houses and computer stores. This program is easy to use and inexpensive. You simply run the program every few weeks to ensure continued good performance from your harddisk.

Incidentally, don't allow smoking around your computers ... they do not like smoke. The microscopic particles in smoke can attach themselves to the surface of your harddisk and potentially cause many problems.

BACKING UP DATA

One of the most heartbreaking events that can occur with your computer is a "harddisk crash."

This means that for any one of a variety of reasons, you can no longer read and recover any data that was stored on your harddisk. In other words, all your data is gone. Someone just took all your filing cabinets! Even with the software maintenance described above, any number of problems (both operator error and equipment malfunctions) can cause your harddisk to crash. Furthermore, it is possible to make a mistake at the keyboard and erase all the data on the disk! This is more than embarrassing or inconvenient ... it can be a disaster. Think about losing ALL your files!

The only way to absolutely ensure you will never lose data is to periodically make and store extra copies of it. Once again, thanks to readily available software, this is easy to do. Unfortunately, it is also easy to FORGET to do it!

TRUISM 26

Sooner or later, when you least expect it, you will lose some or all of the data stored in your computer.

Here is a little reminder:

PERFORM A DAILY BACKUP!

It is not possible to stress this point enough. Loss of data can be a disaster.

You can back up your data in two basic ways. By using a software utility to place copies of your data on diskettes, using a removable storage devide or a tape drive with removable tapes that can be stored away from the machine. As you might expect, the diskette copy method is inexpensive, but a bit more trouble, whereas the removable storage or tape drive approach is quick, easy, and expensive by comparison.

Many backup utilities are available. One of these inexpensive utilities is all you will need for making your daily data backups. This software is available at most computer stores or by mail order. Consider one of the new high-density removable media such as the Zip Drive by Iomega which stores up to 100Mb on a single cartridge. Great for backups and it's very fast!

Whatever backup method you decide to use, backup utility, tape drive, or removable media, ensure that you initially make TWO complete backups of your harddisk and store them in two different locations. You just never know what can happen ... theft, fire, damage. And remember, if you lose your data, IT'S GONE FOREVER. After making this full backup, it is not necessary to make a complete backup each day, you need only backup any files that you have changed that day. Software backup utilities make this very easy by checking each file for a change, and then automatically backing up only that file.

Important Hint: After making your first backup, test it by attempting to recover the data that has been backed up. You don't want to find out that the backup does not work properly when you <u>really</u> need it!

COMPUTER SECURITY

No, I'm not going to tell you to lock up each night. You do that anyway. Furthermore, you better have insurance that covers the loss of your computer. But physical security is not the issue here ... DATA SECURITY is. Your computer will contain most, if not all, of your business records; financial, customer and vendor lists, marketing information, business strategies, planning documents, and more. It is doubtful that you would want certain of this data in the wrong hands. To minimize this possibility, we can again turn to software. Numerous utilities (and some application software) are available that will allow your computer to be used only by authorized personnel with passwords that can be updated and changed from time to time. Furthermore, it is easy to allow certain individuals access to only selected information. This is important since it is likely that different people will use the same computer.

Just like the determined burglar, a determined computer thief can get into your computer in spite of password protection. Additional levels of security are available, if necessary, depending on the sensitivity of your operation. Discussions of these advanced security methods are beyond the scope of this guidebook but computer security consultants are available to assist in this area. For most of us, however, a password is more than adequate.

TRAINING

Part of your employee training program should include computer training covering the various software packages you are using. This training can be done by you or by sending the employee to a short seminar covering the specific software package he or she will be using. Many computer retail stores provide these seminars for the more popular software packages at very reasonable fees. Don't try to save a nickel by giving the employee the manual for the software and telling him to get smart. This will extend the learning curve and you will lose in the long run. Furthermore, it is highly likely the employee will bring back from the seminar a detail or two about the software that is new to you.

CHECKLIST #15: COMPUTER OPERATIONS

☐ Properly train everyone using the computer.

☐ Do not allow anyone to install personal software in your business computer.

☐ Check for virus infection with appropriate software on a regular basis (at least weekly).

☐ Perform backups on a daily basis. Always keep a backup copy away from the business location.

☐ Limit computer access to only those necessary.

☐ Maintain program files and data files in separate directories.

☐ Use password protection.

☐ Perform harddisk maintenance on a regular basis. Follow instructions included with the maintenance software being utilized.

☐ Clean and dust the computer monthly. Use a small vacuum to clean air intake and exhaust locations.

FAX MACHINES

You all know what these are ... an electronic mail box. They are less and less expensive and are becoming nearly indispensable in conducting business. They allow instant transfer of drawings or text to any other FAX machine in the world using your telephone line. Current models, and there are plenty to choose from, produce excellent output. As with all electronic equipment, shop at the discount stores for heavy discounts from "list prices."

FAX machines can be used for regular correspondence and can represent a savings over regular postal service. You save postage, envelopes, administrative time, and you get immediate no-delay delivery! FAX during evening and weekend hours for even more savings by taking advantage of reduced telephone rates.

Another approach to the "traditional" FAX machine is the FAX-Modem card used in conjunction with a personal computer. These cards, along with appropriate software, enable you to send and receive FAX's with the computer. An incoming FAX is simply stored in the computer until you are ready to read it and you send an outgoing FAX by selecting the appropriate file. The major disadvantages of the FAX-Modem card approach are the inability to send unless the data can be stored in the computer and the fact that the computer must be on to receive a FAX.

Caution: FAX transmissions are no more secure than your telephone line. Keep this in mind if you are handling sensitive information. FAX transmissions may be encrypted with appropriate hardware at both the transmitting and receiving end.

Consider the following when selecting your FAX machine:

CHECKLIST #16:
PURCHASING YOUR FAX MACHINE

☐ Does it use plain paper or thermal paper? Plain paper units are more expensive but produce output on regular paper which is easier to read and duplicate.

☐ Does in have a built-in telephone handset? A handy feature.

☐ Are redial and memory functions available?

☐ Is there a copy function? Most do and it's a very handy function for making a quick copy of a few sheets. It is slow, however.

☐ Physical size? Will the unit fit where you plan to place it?

☐ Warranty?

☐ Would a FAX-modem card be a better choice?

COPIERS

You will probably need one. Even with your computer and printer plus the FAX machine copy function, there will be too many times you will need to copy multi-page and odd-sized documents. Copiers are a pain ... they all seem to have problems, so make sure whatever you buy comes with a good guarantee and that repairs will be easy when required. The best advice for selecting a copier is to purchase one with only the features and speed you need ... more speed and features mean more potential problems.

SUMMARY

Using available technology is a must in order to stay competitive in business in today's environment. A personal computer is an example. Get one and learn to use it! It's fun, fairly easy, and a great time saver. Heed the earlier warning about backing up your data. Remember Murphy's law; "If something can go wrong, it will." Your data can be lost in the blink of an eye. Please remember this.

Shop carefully for your other technology needs such as FAX machines, copiers, telephone systems. Do not buy anything fancier than you need and fully understand the vendor's return policy and warranty.

REFERENCES

ITEM	"How To Get Started With A Small Business Computer"
DESCRIPTION	SBA Publication MP15 which contains information for determining your computer needs and selecting the right computer for your business.
WHERE TO OBTAIN	SBA Publications P.O. Box 30 Denver, CO 80201-0030 (202) 205 6665 Most SCORE offices can provide copies of SBA guides.
COST	$0.50 plus $1.00 shipping/handling
COMMENTS	SCORE (Service Corps of Retired Executives) is an SBA affiliate association with offices in most major cities. Refer to your local telephone book.

CHAPTER 14
THE INTERNET

"WE PUT OUR BUSINESS ON THE INTERNET ABOUT HERE..."

One of the most exciting communications, information transfer, and business developments in recent memory is the Internet. You hear about it everywhere—on television and radio, in advertisements, newspapers. For the small business, the Internet can be one of the most effective innovations to come along in years. Why? Because the Internet can give your small business access to a "worldwide" marketplace for a few dollars a month! You can compete head-to-head against the big guys.

The Internet is a giant world-wide network of inter-connected computer networks or "sites" which allows an individual computer connected to this network to access the information on any of the sites on the network. The Internet allows this information to be searched, retrieved and stored by any user. Since many of the connected sites contain a wealth of useful information, the Internet is an important business resource.

You may have read that the Internet is hard to learn and access. Maybe it was at first, but not any more! Along with the astounding growth of the Internet, numerous small "access providers" have sprung up all over the country, many of whom will get you up and running on the Internet quickly and easily. More on this later.

This chapter will introduce you to the Internet but it is not going to make you an expert. To really understand and make use of this resource, you must "get connected" and I'll describe this process below. Also, I urge you to check out some of the references listed in Appendix IV for additional information.

WHAT IS THE INTERNET?

The Internet started around 1969 as a way of connecting government and university computers together for research. It has been growing exponentially ever since. In fact, at this time, estimates put the number of sites worldwide(places you can get information) at around 3 to 5 million! Since each site could have many users, this means that at any moment, <u>millions</u> of individuals are accessing the Internet. The current estimate of growth is 10% per month!

The Internet is a big network of computers talking to one another. None of these computers is in control and there is no "central point" on the

Internet. Amazingly, in spite of its large size, the Internet is a cooperative effort with no one in charge, and it seems to work.

The Internet continues to grow at a phenomenal rate and cannot be ignored as an important and effective resource and sales channel for small business.

INTERNET SPECIFICS

The Internet supports a variety of services, sometimes called applications, utilities, or tools. The most important are:

E-MAIL (electronic mail). This is the most popular Internet application. There are literally tens of millions of E-mail account users worldwide. Using E-mail allows you to send and receive "mail" messages to anyone with an E-mail account. A message may be sent to one person or a number of individuals simultaneously. A message may be a few words or include large text or graphic files as an attachment. Available software makes E-mail very easy to use and in many cases, the software will be free.

> Suggestion: Eudora Light or Eudora Pro by Qualcomm. Eudora Light, is satisfactory for most users and it is free.

Most E-mail messages are delivered within minutes (to anywhere in the world!) and the cost is probably less than sending a letter and certainly less than a telephone call. There is no charge to send E-mail beyond your normal Internet provider's monthly charges. In many cases, E-mail can also replace a FAX.

Think of E-mail as another way to communicate with your customers. Unlike the telephone you don't have to be there to answer the call and no one pays a long distance bill.

Small businesses can use e-mail to take and confirm orders, provide requested product information, announce sales and new products, and provide answers to consumer or customer questions. It is a fantastic resource!

You will be assigned an E-mail address by your Internet provider. For example, my E-mail address is: bobs@isquare.com. Kind of strange looking but you can generally choose the portion prior to the "@." For example, Jonathan Reader might use "jreader@isquare.com"

Your E-mail address should be placed on your letterhead, print advertisements, business cards and anything else that contains your name and postal address.

Note that there is a small possibility that your E-mail messages (not unlike a conversation on a portable or cellular phone) can be intercepted and read. It is normally not a concern but nonetheless you should be aware of the possibility. Software programs are available that will encrypt your messages and make them impossible to read by anyone except the intended recipient.

NEWSGROUPS, sometimes called Internet Discussion Groups are a powerful way to communicate with people around the world who are interested in the same things as you. Currently there are tens of thousands of newsgroups covering every subject imaginable. These groups allow people with like interests to communicate on a worldwide scale.

Any person in the group can send a message to the entire group, and any of the other members can immediately respond to the entire group. Most Internet browsers include a newsgroup reader.

> Suggestion: Use DejaNews to search for newsgroups of interest to you. They can be found on the Internet at http://www.dejanews.com. (See the next paragraph for what these strange characters mean and how to use them)

FTP. This application, File Transfer Protocol, allows you to send or obtain files from many computers on the Internet.

> Suggestion: One of the best FTP programs is WS-FTP by Ipswitch. They can be found on the Internet at http://www.ipswitch.com

WWW. (World Wide Web). This is the big one! The WWW is what everyone is generally referring to when they say, "Internet." It is a graphical interface utilizing hypertext. Hypertext allows you to use your mouse to click on certain highlighted words on the WWW screen which takes you immediately to another place in that document or to another site on the Internet! This is called "linking" and is a very powerful tool.

The WWW uses universal resource locators (URL's) as addresses. For example, my WWW URL address is: http://www.isquare.com). Like "123 Main Street, Mycity, VA., USA", this URL tells the Internet the "street, city, state and country" of the site you would like to be connected to. Most URL's are similar to the company name like "www.fedex.com" for Federal Express. Appendix IV lists some in-teresting and useful URL's for you to try.

See Appendix IV for an example of what a WWW "page" looks like (there really are no 'pages' on the WWW, you simply scroll from beginning to end). If you were reading this example page while connected, every time you saw an underlined phrase, you could immediately link to another WWW site or elsewhere in the same document to obtain further information relating to that topic.

WHY IS THE INTERNET IMPORTANT?

Think about that 5-million number mentioned previously. Quite an audience for your product or service, don't you think? You could, for instance, get an audience this size via television but the cost would probably be prohibitive to you. The good news about the Internet is that access is "free" or very nearly so.

Just a few of the activities available to you as an Internet user include the following:

1. Communicate free with anyone with an Internet E-mail account (there are millions) anywhere in the world and with no long-distance telephone charges!

2. Search and retrieve information from any con-nected computer (there are millions). The information that is available, as you will see, covers virtually every subject imaginable.

3. Conduct test marketing for your product or service.

4. Advertise and market your product or service.

5. Place a catalog of products on the "Net" (a commonly used synonym for the Internet) complete with pictures and descriptions, ordering and contact information, and other details about your products or service.

6. Distribute information to others.

7. Search through thousands of catalogs and offered services.

8. Join one or more of the over 18,000 news and discussion groups covering everything from algebra to zoology.

9. Search for information in libraries, government information services, and various commercial databases.

10. Obtain free software from a variety of sources.

HOW TO GET STARTED

It is easier than you might think. You will, of course, need a computer. There are three major steps to Internet usage:

1. Get connected to the Net
2. Learn to use the Net ("surf" the Net)
3. Create your own presence on the Net

Let's look at each of these in some detail.

Getting Connected. There are four major ways to connect to the Internet—your own connection, the library, a commercial service, or an Internet provider.

1. Your own connection.

   This is not for the small business. This approach requires lots of expensive equipment and expertise.

2. Visit a library.

   This is a neat way to try out the net without spending any money. Many large libraries now have one or more computers connected to the Internet that may be used by visitors. You obviously can't use this approach for your business, but it's a great way to familiarize yourself with the net and see what this tool might mean to you and your business.

3. Use a commercial service.

   The commercial services such as America-On-Line, CompuServe, and Prodigy provide some form of Internet access. The good news is that this approach is an easy and quick way to get on the Net. However, in some cases, Internet access is limited in various ways and you can expect to pay more than with a private Internet service provider. Some people start using a commercial service and once familiar with the Net, switch to an Internet Provider.

4. An Internet Provider.

   This is my preferred approach. It is easy to find a local "access provider" and get an "Internet account" which allows you to connect into the Internet. One way to find these providers is to check in the business section of your local newspaper. Cost is around $10-$20/month which will give you anywhere from a few hours access each day to unlimited access. More good news: Required software for your computer is generally free or very low cost shareware available from the provider (or you can download it from various hosts with help from your provider).

There are different types of Internet accounts that provide various levels of service. Suffice it to say that you will need a "dial-in PPP" account which will allow you to take full advantage of the Internet at a low cost. (PPP stands for Point-to-Point Protocol.)

Be careful when selecting your Internet provider since many are coming in existence to support the demand. Some are good, some are not. The following checklist will help you in making your selection.

CHECKLIST #17:
SELECTING AN INTERNET PROVIDER

☐ How long has the provider been in operation?

☐ What are monthly costs? Is access unlimited?

☐ How many access telephone lines are available? Will you be able to easily connect at anytime?

☐ Is a local access telephone number available? (You don't want to incur long-distance charges since you will find that you're spending hours connected!)

☐ Are 28.8 Kbps modems (at a minimum) being used for dial-in accounts? Is ISDN available?

☐ Are personalized E-mail addresses available? You want this for identification. It is your "name" on the Internet. For example, my E-mail address is "bobs@isquare.com. "bobs" is what I've chosen for my "name," "isquare" is the internet "domain" (different for each provider), and "com" indicates a commercial service.

☐ Will software be provided? (It usually is).

☐ Are there any restrictions on doing business using your account?

☐ Is technical help available? During what times? (This assistance should be free.)

☐ What services are offered? You must have E-mail and FTP at a minimum. Will the provider be able to support your "home page" when you're ready?

☐ Are there any setup or activation fees?

☐ How much disk space will you receive with your account? You should have at least 2Mb if you are going to have a webpage.

☐ Shop around! Compare prices!

Equipment Required.

Hopefully, you have decided that a computer is an absolute necessity for your business. Given that you already have or will get a computer, the only additional piece of equipment required to support Internet access is a modem. This is the device that connects your computer to the telephone line. It is very important that this modem be able to transfer lots of data quickly. Fortunately, the cost of modems has come down considerably and for around $150 you can add a 28.8Kbps modem to your computer. "28.8Kbps" defines how fast the modem transfers data and is the minimum speed you should use with the Internet for satisfactory performance.

Learn to use the Net.

At this point a lot of what you have read in this section may be confusing but believe me, once you get connected and start using the various tools we've described, everything will start to make sense.

When you are up and running on the Internet, start looking around using your various applications (called "surfing the Net") and get familiar with what's there. You will quickly be amazed at what is available and the possibilities. Send us an E-mail! (bobs@isquare.com)

Create your own presence on the Net.

Using the Internet to advertise your product or service is considerably different than traditional sales and promotional techniques. The bad news is that you must stand out in a crowd of millions! The good news is that you can "look" like a company that sells millions! To do so requires you to carefully think through your strategy to ensure whatever you place on the Net is very unique and interesting.

When using the Net to advertise, and again contrary to the traditional advertising, you must give to the Net as well as use its capabilities. In other words, your advertising must also provide useful information to the reader. An example of this is the sample Internet page of Appendix IV. Notice that, as well as advertising services (consulting and books), information for finding additional resources is also included.

The form of your presence on the Net is dependent on your business goals and marketing specifics. A variety of possibilities are described in many excellent references for doing business on the Internet. Refer to Appendix IV.

The major unwritten rule for advertising on the Internet is to NEVER send information to specific individuals that is unsolicited.

You should learn more about the Internet and see how it might fit into your business. Refer to Appendix IV for some suggested reference material. Visit your local bookstore or library and browse through dozens of books that discuss the Internet.

CHAPTER 15
LEARN TO COMMUNICATE

"I FORGOT, DOES ONE GRUNT MEAN 'YES' OR 'NO'?"

Considering how important written and oral communications are in the business world, it is amazing how little attention is given to these areas. Furthermore, most of us are not too good at either. However, it is encouraging to note that improvements in speaking and writing are easy to achieve and can pay big dividends. This chapter will focus on suggestions for improving your performance in both these areas.

WRITING

Your business success will rely to some extent on your ability to write; so it is important that you assess your talents in this area. <u>The purpose of</u>

writing is simply to EFFECTIVELY convey a message to the recipient ... no more and no less. The process has somehow gotten completely out of hand. If you don't believe me, take out one of your insurance policies and try to read it. Is the message clear? If you want a real chuckle, get hold of a government regulation ... any regulation ... and try to understand the message. Can't do it?

You must write clearly and not obfuscate (see what I mean?) the message, since your business survival depends to a great extent on making yourself understood. This chapter provides some tips for making your message understandable.

WRITING GUIDELINES

Think first, then write. EVERYTHING you put on paper becomes a permanent (and legal) record. You cannot take back what you have written and mailed or faxed. Never write when you're angry. In all cases, if time permits, write your message, then come back to it the next day for another quick review. It is true that everything looks different with the morning light.

Keep the recipient in mind. Keep in mind who is to get the message and adjust your text and writing style accordingly. Correspondence to a customer should always be friendly and upbeat even when discussing a problem.

> Wrong: "Our warranty clearly states that no returns will be accepted after 60 days. After that time the manufacturer is responsible for any repairs."

> Better: "I am sorry you are having problems with your lawn mower. As you know we do not

accept returns after 60 days. As noted in the manual, you can return the mower to the manufacturer for repairs. And, because we value you as a customer, we will be happy to loan you our demonstration unit until yours is returned."

Now, make certain there is a big sign on the side of the mower that states, "Loaner courtesy ABC Company." You get free advertising in your customer's neighborhood.

Make your message as personal as possible ... it makes you more believable.

Wrong: "We at XYZ will remain committed to serving you in the future."

Better: "I hope to see you in the store again soon."

Understand the purpose for the communications. Include only what is required for clarity. In other words, don't beat around the bush. Your reader is looking for a certain message ... present that message early in the text, before the reader becomes bored.

Wrong. "We appreciate the opportunity to ... blah blah ... XYZ has been in business for ... and we have furnished similar ... blah blah ... Attachment 1 lists your cost for the items requested."

Better. "Ref: Your request for pricing dated April 2, 1992. [chart of prices]. Thank you and please call with any questions."

People are busy, just like you are, and do not want to be entertained by correspondence. They just want answers.

Obtain an independent review. If possible, have someone review your correspondence for understanding and clarity. The message may be obvious to you and no one else. There is a story told that Napoleon had his "dullest" foot soldier read all his directives before they were sent to his generals. His thought was that if this foot soldier understood the message, there was no chance that anyone else would misinterpret his orders.

Proofread. It is amazing how many errors can be found in correspondence. When this happens you immediately lose credibility with the reader. Never mind how the error crept in ... it is now too late. Proofread thoroughly. Do NOT rely on your word processor's spell checker ... it cannot interpret what you are trying to say. For example it cannot make the correct decision with respect to words like there/their, for/four, capitol/capital.

Do not rely on any of the software "grammar checkers." They are simply not good enough (yet) to be effective and you cannot afford mistakes. "Sorry, Mr. Jones, but apparently my computer did not understand what I was trying to say."

Write deductively. In other words, make your point immediately and follow up with the supporting facts. This allows the reader to get to the point before losing interest. This ties in with understanding the purpose of the communications as discussed above.

Organize your writing. Start with an outline and then fill in the specifics. In that manner, you will be assured of an organized document.

Now for a few specific Dos and Don'ts for your correspondence. These ideas are not new and are expanded upon in the resource material listed at the end of the chapter.

CHECKLIST #18: WRITING GUIDELINES

☐ <u>Do</u> pay attention to detail. Your correspondence should be neat with correct spelling, grammar usage, and punctuation.

☐ <u>Do</u> organize your material to present a clear message.

☐ <u>Do</u> be precise. Use words with exact meanings.

☐ <u>Do</u> use humor, if it's appropriate, and especially if the subject is dull ... it will help to keep the reader's attention.

☐ <u>Don't</u> be verbose. Read any legal document for examples of this!

☐ <u>Don't</u> try to impress the reader with big complex words. Just clearly state your message.

The best way to learn to write is to write. Practice! Write letters to companies and ask for literature, begin a daily diary, write to your mother.

SPEAKING

There are many situations where speaking effectively will make the difference between winning and losing. Most of us rarely consider how we speak or if our message is being perceived correctly.

Every book written about speaking in various situations never fails to mention that speaking in front of an audience is everyone's number one fear (perhaps even edging out death!). Maybe that's true, and with a few pointers, it is amazing how easy and, yes, enjoyable, public speaking can be.

Incidentally, an audience of ONE should be treated no differently than an auditorium full of people.

Arch Lustberg's book, "Winning When It Really Counts" is an absolute must reference on speaking (See reference listing at end of chapter). It contains a wealth of excellent tips for effective speaking in a number of different situations. Many of the comments presented here are expanded upon in his book.

When you are speaking, all eyes will be on you! Therefore, everything, both audible and visual becomes important. Your audience, whether one or many, is listening to the inflections and tone of your voice and watching your body language and your facial expressions. You will feel like you cannot afford even a little mistake in either word or gesture. This is probably one of the reasons everyone is so nervous about speaking. The answer to alleviating your fears in this situation is easier than you might think: Be aware of a few basic rules of speaking and then practice. The checklist that follows contains a variety of simple and effective techniques that you can use to get spoken messages across effectively.

CHECKLIST #19: SPEAKING GUIDELINES

☐   Dress for the occasion but make sure you are comfortable. Look in a mirror before going "on stage." Hair okay? Nothing on your teeth? Fly zipped up? Practice a smile and take a few deep breaths.

☐ Smile at your audience, when appropriate.

☐ Do not be afraid to gesture ... it is a great technique for emphasizing a point. But don't overdue it to the point where you are always in motion which can be distracting to the listeners.

☐ Talk in a conversational tone. Don't "lecture."

☐ PREPARE. This is obvious and too important not to mention. If you are prepared you will exude self-confidence which will be apparent to the audience. Preparation means researching so you understand your topic.

☐ PRACTICE. Practice until you are satisfied with your delivery.

☐ Speak clearly, not too fast, with appropriate inflection, and keep your text simple. Big, impressive words are not necessary and can be distracting when your audience tries to figure out what they mean.

☐ Make sure your message is organized, clear, and to the point.

☐ Stand (or sit) tall. Maintain a leadership bearing, erect and leaning slightly forward.

☐ Maintain eye contact with your audience. Observe other speakers and note how often they are speaking to something other than their listeners. It is very distracting to an audience to have a speaker address the ceiling or podium!

☐ Use the pause effectively. A second or two of silence is preferred over three or four "uh" or "ums." The stuttering speech that results from those little "uh" and "um" sounds drive listeners crazy and makes it sound like you don't know your material. You lose credibility. So don't do it. Simply pause!

- ☐ Do not argue or become confrontational with anyone in your audience. If someone gives you a hard time, do your best to ignore it or offer to speak with them at the end of your delivery.

- ☐ Be honest. If you don't know something, simply say "I don't know."

- ☐ Be yourself. If you put on an act, you lose sincerity and credibility.

SUMMARY

The importance of communication cannot be over emphasized. Learn to write clearly and speak effectively. Follow the basic rules presented above and practice. Keep your written messages personal and to the point. Deliver your spoken messages with sincerity ... be yourself and be honest.

REFERENCES

ITEM	"The Secretary's Handbook" 10th Edition by Taintor and Monro.
DESCRIPTION	Published by MacMillan. An excellent and extensive text. Covers grammar, English usage, spelling, proof-reading
WHERE TO OBTAIN	Bookstores, Library

ITEM	"Winning When It Really Counts" by Arch Lustberg
DESCRIPTION	Published by Simon and Schuster. Contains strategies for effective speaking.
WHERE TO OBTAIN	Bookstores, Library
COST	$17.95

ITEM	"Webster's Guide to Business Correspondence"
DESCRIPTION	Published by Merriam-Webster. A major reference work covering a wide variety of business writing skills.
WHERE TO OBTAIN	Bookstores, Library

ITEM	"English for Modern Business," 4th ed by Richard Irwin.
DESCRIPTION	A grammar textbook with plenty of examples.
WHERE TO OBTAIN	Bookstores, Library, or from Richard Irwin, 1818 Ridge Road, Homewood, Il 60430
COST	$15.00

ITEM	SBA Effective Business Communication MP 1
DESCRIPTION	Describes the importance of business communications with specific suggestions and a useful bibliography.
WHERE TO OBTAIN	SBA Publications P.O. Box 30 Denver, CO 80201-0030 (202) 205 6665 Most SCORE offices can provide copies of SBA guides.
COST	$0.50
COMMENTS	SCORE (Service Corps of Retired Executives) is an SBA affiliate association with offices in most major cities. Refer to your local telephone book.

ITEM	"Technically Speaking: Proven Ways to Make Your Next Presentation a Success" by Jan D'Arcy
DESCRIPTION	Excellent text on speaking ... many good hints.
WHERE TO OBTAIN	Amacom 135 W. 50th Street New York, NY 10020 Also check library and book stores
COST	$28.95

CHAPTER 16
DAY TO DAY OPERATIONS

"HARRIS, YOU'VE BEEN TRADED TO MARKETING FOR TWO OFFICE CHAIRS AND A STAPLER."

This chapter is a listing of a wide variety of suggestions that are based on the business experiences of a number of small business owners. They range from light-hearted to very serious and all contain a good deal of wisdom. You will surely find a few to be useful in your own business. Topics are divided into the following major categories:

- Saving Money
- Selling Your Product or Service
- Selling Yourself
- Telephone Usage

SAVING MONEY

What do you think is easier to do ... reduce your expenses by 5% or double your sales? I think most would agree that reducing expenses might be easier. In spite of this most business owners spend very little time on attempting to reduce expenses. Consider this: Your current profit margin is 5% - if you reduce costs by 5% your profits double!

It is amazingly simple to reduce operating costs a few percent by being diligent. The following checklist will presents a number of money-saving ideas. You may find that you can reduce spending by observing only a few of the suggestions. And remember, the small stuff adds up! Think about saving each time you spend and you will discover your own ways to save.

CHECKLIST #20: SAVING MONEY

☐ Negotiate EVERYthing, including services. You can frequently purchase at a discount by merely asking. Always request a discount if you pay in cash or if you intend to pay within 5-10 days.

> ### TRUISM 27
> Negotiating will save you money.

☐ Shop by mail order when applicable ... it is frequently economical and convenient. Use a credit card for your mail order purchases. The credit card company will assist you if you have a problem with the mail order firm whereas you have little recourse if you pay by check.

☐ Shop and compare for all your needs. This is especially true if you are in the manufacturing business where prices for goods can vary widely. Don't get locked into a single vendor. For example, if you have been purchasing office supplies from the same supplier for a few months, put your normal order up for bid with their competitors...it is likely you will do better. Of course, there are intangibles to consider such as service, quality and convenience in your decision to switch suppliers.

☐ Toll free calling can add up to significant telephone service savings. Numerous vendors and suppliers have toll-free 800 numbers which may not be widely advertised. Don't purchase an expensive "800 directory" from one of the long distance carriers. A more economical way to check on the availability of an 800 number is to simply dial (800) 555-1212 for the "800" operator, who will have listings for all carriers. Another alternative is to use the Internet to search 800 numbers (See Appendix IV).

☐ Keep a close watch on energy consumption. Auto-setback thermostats and automatic light switches can be used to conserve energy at low cost. Both of these items can quickly pay for themselves in energy savings.

☐ Use FAX or E-mail instead of mail. This way you save postage, envelope, paper, mailing time and get instant delivery. Transmit in the evenings or on weekends for reduced telephone rates and even more savings.

☐ Barter, if possible. It can work under the right circumstances.

> The soldering machinery I used in my electronics manufacturing business had a utilization factor of about 30%. This expensive equipment sat idle 70% of the work week. As luck would have it, the company that provided me with printed circuit layout service (CAD, or computer aided design) had a similar problem with their expensive CAD equipment. We set up a barter arrangement in which I would provide soldering services for those cases when his customers required manufacturing services and, in return, I received CAD services. We bartered on a case-by-case basis. The result was increased utilization of our expensive equipment, which would otherwise sit idle.

☐ Shop for the best telephone service. Services AND rates vary considerably and a little investigation can bring big savings. Consider a WATS line if you do a lot of long distance calling to specific areas of the country. A WATS line is quite inexpensive if you only use a few calling areas. On the other hand a "nationwide" WATS service is quite expensive.

☐ Monitor telephone usage and office supplies (including the postage meter, if used). Telephones and office supplies are often misused (usually unknowingly) and considerable savings are possible by being diligent. You, the owner, are the person most concerned with savings, and so it is up to you to keep an eye on ALL expenses.

> During an expense review of my manufacturing business (10 employees), I noted we were spending an average of $1200 a month for "office supplies." I was shocked! Where was it going? I did a "Sunday morning audit" and found, in the assembly area alone, over 100 pens and no less than 50 partially used hard cover tablets, a dozen staplers, and probably a years worth of other miscellaneous supplies. Only five people worked in assembly. What was happening, was that no one kept track of anything, and every time a pen or tablet was needed a quick trip to the supply cabinet was made. The office helper, periodically checking supplies, would (correctly) restock the cabinet! We subsequently locked the cabinet, issued supplies when requested, and kept a log. This may be a trivial example, but these kind of things get overlooked during the pressure of daily business and can cost a small company big money. In this case, a $7.00 lock on the cabinet and a minor procedure change saved hundreds of dollars per month.

☐ <u>Buy used or reconditioned</u>. Tremendous saving is possible by purchasing used equipment, furniture, tools, and other business related items. Check local want-ads, auctions, business close-outs, and Internet buy/sell listings for great savings. Remember, no warranties will apply so be on your toes and do your homework. Know what to look for, make sure you know what you are buying and know the items actual ("street") cost. You are in a better negotiating position with this information.

☐ <u>Plan shipping or mailings</u> to avoid overnight or second day delivery that is MUCH more expensive than alternate methods. If you must ship overnight check the various carriers as well as the post office for the best rates.

SELLING YOUR PRODUCT OR SERVICE

Make it easy for the customer! In these busy times, the customer's choice to purchase may be based on how easy it is to make the purchase rather than price. Here are a few ideas to make your product or service easy for customers to purchase.

CHECKLIST #21:
SELLING YOUR PRODUCT OR SERVICE

☐ Accept credit cards for purchase. See Appendix V for details on obtaining a merchant card account and how to assess the provider.

☐ Provide a money-back policy.

☐ Distribute free catalogues.

☐ Get an 800 number for sales AND service. Ensure the number is well attended.

☐ Provide a guarantee for your goods or services and back it up!

☐ Give away something free from time to time.

☐ Provide limited free after-sale assistance.

☐ If you're in the retail business, maintain store hours in the evenings and on weekends.

☐ Provide a delivery service (or service at the customer's location).

☐ Follow up sales to the extent possible. Personal calls for big ticket sales and a returnable post card for higher volume sales, for example.

☐ Have a "preferred customer" sale.

SELLING YOURSELF

As important as it is to make your product or service easy to sell, you must also sell yourself. In your role as entrepreneur you must make customers want to buy from you, convince your banker you are a good risk, show your competitors you are a force to be reckoned with. In short, you must show the world you are successful and a winner! You and your business must look successful. Here are some tips:

CHECKLIST #22: SELLING YOURSELF

☐ Always dress the part. Dark, stylish suits or dresses when conducting business. Clean work clothes (with company logo) when in the "shop."

☐ Get involved in community activities, especially if your business provides services to the community. Your name will get around as someone who is interested in community affairs.

☐ Drive the nicest car you can afford and keep it clean. Like it or not, the car you drive says a lot about your success.

☐ Keep your business establishment clean and tidy, no matter what the business. Keep everything neat and orderly. Direct your employees to keep it that way. A neat and orderly work place breeds efficiency and customer confidence!

> An acquaintance started an engine re-building business in a small bay of a warehouse. The location was good in terms of convenience and deliveries of materials but the bay itself was typical. Cinder block from floor to ceiling, open metal roof girders with hanging industrial florescent fixtures. Although my friend had an excellent reputation and was an excellent engine man, business stunk! We literally turned business around overnight by painting the entire place brilliant white (including the ceiling and girders), painting bright graphics on the walls, organizing everything in the place, and holding an open house. Suddenly it was the place to go for engine work. The business <u>looked</u> successful.

TRUISM 28
A successful business looks successful.

☐ If your business is home-based, project professionalism. Here are a few hints:

1. Have a separate work area where "household" noises will not interfere with business.

2. A separate telephone line is mandatory (with an answering machine).

3. The name of your business should be chosen so as to give a professional image. If you're baking and selling cookies out of your Alden Hills home, don't call yourself "Doris' Home Grown Cookies." A better choice might be "Alden Hills Bakery."

4. If possible, have a separate entrance for your business. This is convenient for both clients and deliveries.

A friend of mine neatly solved this problem by remodeling half of his double garage into an office. He used a separate door into the garage as his "business entrance." Everyone was happy with the arrangement. He has a separate, quiet place to work with a separate entrance and his family again have the den and one bedroom which he had previously used for the business.

---

5. Be prepared for visitors. Have refreshments available. Ensure your office area is always neat and clean. In short, be a good host — make your visitors (read, "customers!") comfortable.

TELEPHONE USAGE

Don't become a slave to your telephone. It can be both the greatest convenience and inconvenience ever invented. The telephone is for YOUR use, not the CALLER'S. Your telephone should never interrupt you. Use a good answering machine or voice mail if you cannot pick up immediately.

CHECKLIST #23: TELEPHONE USAGE

☐ Make all conversations as brief as possible. Get to the point quickly and stick to it. By all means, be courteous but help the caller stick to the subject. The telephone can be a great time waster.

☐ Make use of current telephone system technology. Time saving features include call waiting, call forwarding, auto-dialing with number memory. Fancier systems include useful extras such as, call-cost display which keeps a running total of cost of the current call, break-in to let another worker deliver a message to you without your caller hearing it, toll restrictions to prevent unauthorized long-distance usage, and various call cost reporting reports that can be very useful in auditing telephone usage.

☐ Don't let the telephone ring more than two times before picking up.

☐ If you use an answering machine or voice mail, make the announcement as short as possible. For example: "Thanks for calling Information International. No one is available at the moment, please call back or leave a message. Thank you." No one likes to listen to a 2-minute message which gives information like addresses, other telephone numbers that may be used, names of people, details on how to leave the message (everyone knows to wait for the "beep!"), hours of operation, or the next vacation day you will be closed.

☐ If possible, answer your own telephone ... it's a wonderful personal touch. If you do have the services of a secretary, do NOT play the "who's going get on the line first" game. It is a waste of time and an irritant to the calling party.

SUMMARY

The little things can make a big difference when operating a business. Be observant and pay attention to the details. Your return for this diligence will be happier customers and higher profits.

> Work is life, you know, and without it, there's
> nothing but fear and insecurity
> ... John Lennon

CHAPTER 17 CONCLUSION

If you have read to this point (starting from the front of the book, that is), you have gained an appreciation of many areas of potential concern with respect to starting and running a business. You have also learned that there is a LOT of good information and help available that is, for the most part, inexpensive (or free) and easy to obtain. Hopefully what you have read has helped you decide if starting a business is right for you and what to expect. If so, great!

The following chart is a review and reminder of the chronology of steps described throughout this book that are considered necessary for starting and running your business successfully.

STEP #	DESCRIPTION	TEXT REFERENCES
One	Assess your aptitude as an entrepreneur	Chapter 2 Checklist #1
Two	Choose your business wisely	Chapter 3 Checklist #2
Three	Choose the legal structure of your business. Discuss with your attorney and accountant	Chapter 3 Chapter 7 Checklist #5
Four	Investigate the legal requirements associated with your specific business	Chapter 3 Checklist #3
Five	Determine financial needs	Chapter 4
Six	Consider a partner for your business	Chapter 5 Checklist #4
Seven	Prepare a strategic plan	Chapter 6

(cont)

Eight	Discuss the business with your banker and establish a personal relationship	Chapter 8 Checklist #7
Nine	Layout a marketing plan	Chapter 10 Checklists #8 & #9
Ten	Protect yourself against liability	Chapter 11 Checklists #10 & #11
Eleven	Understand your responsibilities before deciding to hire employees	Chapter 12 Checklist #12
Twelve	Get a computer and learn to use it	Chapter 13, 14 Checklists #13 & #14
Thirteen	Assess your writing and speaking skills. Improve, if necessary	Chapter 15 Checklists #16 & #17
Fourteen	Okay, now open your door for business. Remember, it is up to you to keep an eye on everything!	Chapter 16 Checklists #19 thru #21
Fifteen	Revisit your strategic plan	Chapter 6

CHECKLIST #24: SUMMARY POINTERS

☐ **Get smart.**

Take advantage of the information available as well as the various support organizations such as the SBA and SCORE.

☐ **Get advice.**

Use as many sources as possible. Talk to your attorney, accountant and banker. Talk to your friends, family and your competition.

☐ **Plan**.

If you do not understand the importance of planning by this time, we have failed. Return to page one and start again!

☐ **Protect yourself.**

Before you start operations, make certain you are protected from a legal and insurance point of view. Take NO chances!

☐ **Avoid hiring employees at the start.**

This is not always possible and, if you will be hiring, make certain you understand the rules.

☐ **Purchase a computer and learn to use it.**

It is almost mandatory for you to be competitive in just about any business.

☐ **Persist.**

There will be good times and hard times so be persistent and stubborn, if necessary.

☐ **Visualize success.**

Keep your goals in mind and expect that you will achieve them. Don't lose sight of your goal...keep pushing.

And finally...

☐ **Don't delay acting on a good idea.**

Even a great idea is worthless if you don't do something with it.

Good luck and good business!

Any comments you may have on this book would be appreciated. We've done our best to provide accurate information and regret any errors that may have crept in. Also, some telephone numbers may have changed. We would like to hear from you if you have any corrections or comments. Correspondence from readers is always welcomed.

Information International
Box 579, Great Falls, VA 22066
(703) 450 7049 voice
(703) 450 7394 FAX

e-mail: bobs@isquare.com
Internet URL: http://www.isquare.com

APPENDIX I
GENERAL REFERENCE

The reference listings in this section supplement the individual chapter listings and are included here so you can easily determine how this material may be obtained. The listings are organized into the following major areas:

- General Business Assistance & Information
- Computers & Software
- Finance
- Patents, Trademarks, Copyrights

General Business Assistance and Information

ITEM	"Small Business Reporter"
DESCRIPTION	Information of assistance to the small business owner or potential owner in such areas as business operations; professional management; and business profiles for endeavors such as the handicrafts business & gift stores.
WHERE TO OBTAIN	Small Business Reporter Bank of America, Dept. 3631 P.O. Box 37000 San Francisco, CA 94137 (415) 622-2491
COST	Call for fee information.
COMMENTS	Some of the business operation topics include—how to buy or sell a business, financing small business, management succession, and understanding financial statements.

ITEM	Service Corps of Retired Executives (SCORE®)
DESCRIPTION	A program of the Small Business Administration (SBA) which matches retired volunteers with small businesses that need expert advice.
WHERE TO OBTAIN	National SCORE® Office 409 3rd Street, SW, Suite 5900 Washington, DC 0024-3212 (202) 205-6762
COST	Free.

ITEM	Small Business Development Centers (SBDC)
DESCRIPTION	Organized by the U.S. Small Business Administration (SBA) to deliver up-to-date counseling, training, and research assistance in all aspects of small business management. The program, available to present and prospective small business owners, offers "one-stop" assistance in central and easily accessible locations.
WHERE TO OBTAIN	Small Business Administration (800) 827-5722 or Assn. of Small Business Development Centers 1313 Farnam on the Mall, Suite 132 Omaha, NE 68182-0472 (402) 595-2387
COST	Free.

ITEM	"Small Business Success"
DESCRIPTION	An annually updated pamphlet that includes tips on such topics as surviving an economic downturn; getting a bank loan; selling a business; automating your company; shopping for a FAX machine; etc.
WHERE TO OBTAIN	Pacific Bell Directory 101 Spear Street Attn: Communications Dept. P-CWS4, Room 429 San Francisco, CA 94105
COST	Free.
COMMENTS	Developed with the Small Business Administration

ITEM	"Starting and Operating a Business in (state)"
DESCRIPTION	Large size paperback covering current Federal and state laws that affect businesses. Many samples of government forms and where to obtain assistance. Includes sections on business legal forms, buying an existing business, starting a business, operating the business, and specific state laws. Separate book for each state.
WHERE TO OBTAIN	PSI Research, Inc., 300 North Valley Drive, Grants Pass, OR 97526 (800) 228 2275 FAX (503) 476 1479
COST	$21.95
COMMENTS	Highly recommended, up-to-date reference

ITEM	Small Business Incubator (SBI) Centers
DESCRIPTION	Incubators are business-assistance programs that provide fledgling business owners with affordable space, office support services, and management and financial assistance. The tenants (small businesses) share meeting space and ideas.
WHERE TO OBTAIN	National Business Incubation Association 1 President Street Athens, OH 45701 (614) 593-4331
COST	Information is free.

ITEM	"Small Business Directory"
DESCRIPTION	A list of the U.S. Small Business Administration (SBA) publications and videotapes on starting and managing a small business.
WHERE TO OBTAIN	U.S. Small Business Administration Small Business Directory P.O. Box 1000 Ft. Worth, TX 76119 (800) 827-5722
COST	The directory is free.
COMMENTS	The publications range in price from $.50 to $2.00 each and the videotapes cost about $30.00 each.

ITEM	U.S. Small Business Administration (SBA)
DESCRIPTION	An agency of the U.S. Gov't created to help entrepreneurs form successful enterprises.
WHERE TO OBTAIN	The SBA has offices located around the country. For the nearest one, consult the telephone directory under U.S. Government, or call the Small Business Answer Desk. (800) U ASK SBA (827-5722)
COST	General information is free.

ITEM	"The Startup Guide" by David Bangs, Jr.
DESCRIPTION	A handbook describing in chronological order all the actions to be taken in planning for your business startup
WHERE TO OBTAIN	Upstart Publishing Co. 12 Portland Street, Dover, NH 03820. (800) 235 8866
COST	$18.95
COMMENTS	Other useful manuals are also available. Ask for a catalog.

ITEM	"How to Set up Your Own Small Business," by Max Fallek
DESCRIPTION	A two volume set containing a LOT of good information.
WHERE TO OBTAIN	Library or the American Institute of Small Business, 7515 Wayzata Blvd., Suite 201, Minneapolis, MN 55426 (612) 545 7001
COST	Call or write for information.

Computers and Software

ITEM	Software: "The Small Business Expert" by Michael Jenkins
DESCRIPTION	An expert program designed to aid and advise the small business owner with respect to tax, legal, and other business questions. Contains many interesting and useful features
WHERE TO OBTAIN	PSI Research, 300 North Valley Drive, Grants Pass, OR 97526. (800) 228 2275 FAX (503) 476 1479
COST	$59.95
COMMENTS	Other business software is available

ITEM	Computer Software - "Cash Flow Analysis"
DESCRIPTION	A software program that has been tested and approved by the U.S. SBA.
WHERE TO OBTAIN	National Business Association Dallas, TX (800) 456-0440
COST	$5.00 (includes shipping)
COMMENTS	This is a bare-bones product. There are no manuals to explain it, just a few instructions on how to get started, printed on the disk envelope or on a separate sheet of paper. It is easy to install and to use, with on-screen instructions to guide you.

ITEM	Computer Software - "First Step Review"
DESCRIPTION	This software program is designed to help assess your chances of obtaining a U.S. Small Business Administration (SBA) guaranteed loan. Versions are available for both IBM-compatible and Macintosh computers.
WHERE TO OBTAIN	National Business Association Dallas, TX (800) 456-0440
COST	Free.
COMMENTS	This is a bare-bones product. There are no manuals to explain it, just a few instructions on how to get started, printed on the disk envelope or on a separate sheet of paper. It's easy to install and to use, with on-screen instructions to guide you. It has been tested and approved by the U.S. SBA.

ITEM	"VenCap Data Quest"
DESCRIPTION	A software program that allows you to search through a listing of venture capital firms who might be interested in your particular product.
WHERE TO OBTAIN	(800) 677-7760
COST	$90.00
COMMENTS	Program is updated every three months.

ITEM	Computer Software - "Business Plan"
DESCRIPTION	A software program that has been tested and approved by the U.S. SBA.
WHERE TO OBTAIN	National Business Association Dallas, TX (800) 456-0440
COST	$5.00 (includes shipping)
COMMENTS	This is a bare-bones product. There are no manuals to explain it, just a few instructions on how to get started, printed on the disk envelope or on a separate sheet of paper. It is easy to install and to use, with on-screen instructions to guide you.

ITEM	Computer Software - "Projected Profit or Loss Statement"
DESCRIPTION	A software program that has been tested and approved by the U.S. SBA.
WHERE TO OBTAIN	National Business Association Dallas, TX (800) 456-0440
COST	$5.00 (includes shipping)
COMMENTS	This is a bare-bones product. There are no manuals to explain it, just a few instructions on how to get started, printed on the disk envelope or on a separate sheet of paper. It is easy to install and to use, with on-screen instructions to guide you.

Finance

ITEM	Various SBA Publications
DESCRIPTION	FM1: ABC's of Borrowing FM2: Profit Costing And Pricing for Manufacturers FM3: Basic Budgets For Profit Planning FM4: Understanding Cash Flow FM5: A Venture Capital Primer For Small Business FM6: Accounting Services For Small Service Firms FM7: Analyze Your Records To Reduce Costs FM8: Budgeting In A Small Service Firm FM9: Sound Cash Management And Borrowing FM10: Record Keeping In A Small Business FM11: Simple Break-Even Analysis For Small Stores FM12: Retailers Pricing checklist FM13: Pricing Your Products And Services Profitably Most SCORE offices can provide copies of SBA guides
WHERE TO OBTAIN	SBA Publications, P. O. Box 30, Denver, CO 80201-0030 (202) 205 6665
COST	$0.50 or $1.00 each plus $1.00 shipping/handling
COMMENTS	SCORE (Service Corps of Retired Executives) is an SBA affiliate association with offices in most major cities. Refer to your local telephone book.

Patents, Trademarks, and Copyrights

ITEM	"Patent Attorneys and Agents Registered to Practice Before the U.S. Patent and Trademark Office"
DESCRIPTION	Listing of patent attorneys.
WHERE TO OBTAIN	U.S. Patent and Trademark Office; Washington, DC 20231 (703) 557-4636; or, U.S. Government Printing Office Washington, DC 20402 (202) 783-3238
COST	Free.

ITEM	Listing of information pamphlets and booklets published by the U.S. Patent and Trademark Office
DESCRIPTION	This listing includes such publications as "Basic Facts About Patents" and "General Information Concerning Patents."
WHERE TO OBTAIN	U.S. Patent and Trademark Office, Washington, DC 20231 (703) 557-4636
COST	Free.

ITEM	"How to Profit from Your Ideas"
DESCRIPTION	A step-by-step guide that shows how you can make money by turning your creative ideas into marketable products. A resource guide for entrepreneurs.
WHERE TO OBTAIN	Flemming Bank & Associates P.O. Box 20365 Portland, OR 97220
COST	$12.95

ITEM	NIST Evaluation Program
DESCRIPTION	The National Institute of Standards and Technology (NIST) provides a technical evaluation program oriented specifically to the needs of inventors and innovators. This program places an emphasis on technical evaluations of energy-related inventions and acts as a screening and referral agency for the Department of Energy (DOE). The DOE may provide funding for those inventions referred by NIST.
WHERE TO OBTAIN	National Institute of Standards and Technology (NIST), Office of Energy-Related Inventions (OERI) Gaithersburg, MD 20899 (301) 975-5500
COST	Free.
COMMENTS	The NIST evaluation program is a lengthy process which recommends about 1½ % of the submissions it receives to DOE. DOE, however, funds many of those recommended.

ITEM	Inventor Information
DESCRIPTION	General information related to energy and environmental matters.
WHERE TO OBTAIN	Argonne National Laboratory Inventor-Assistance Program Building 372 Argonne, IL 60439 (312) 972-3738
COST	Call for information.

ITEM	Inventor Information
DESCRIPTION	General information and workshops oriented to meet the needs of independent inventors and technological entrepreneurs.
WHERE TO OBTAIN	Inventor's Workshop International 3201 Corte Malpaso, #304 Camarillo, CA 93010 (805) 484-9786
COST	Call for information.

ITEM	Inventor Information
DESCRIPTION	A source of assistance for independent inventors and technological entrepreneurs.
WHERE TO OBTAIN	National Appropriate Technology Assistance Program P.O. Box 2525 Butte, MT 59702-2525 (800) 428-2525
COST	Call for information.

ITEM	Inventor Information
DESCRIPTION	A source of information for independent inventors.
WHERE TO OBTAIN	National Clearing House for Innovation Center for Business Research and Development Southwest Missouri State University Springfield, MO 65804-0089 (417) 487-4600
COST	Call for information.

ITEM	Inventor Information
DESCRIPTION	A source for inventors or innovators to obtain a commercial evaluation of their product or idea.
WHERE TO OBTAIN	Center for Innovation and Business Development University of North Dakota Box 8103, University Station Grand Forks, ND 58202 (701) 777-3132
COST	Call for information.

ITEM	Inventor Information
DESCRIPTION	A source for inventors or innovators to obtain a commercial evaluation of their product or idea.
WHERE TO OBTAIN	Innovation Institute Rt. 2, Box 124, Everton, MO 65646 (417) 836-5680
COST	Call for information.

ITEM	"Submitting An Idea"
DESCRIPTION	A publication that describes the usual procedures involved in submitting an idea to a company.
WHERE TO OBTAIN	American Bar Association Circulation Department 750 North Shore Lake Drive Chicago, IL 60611 (312) 988 5000
COST	Call for price.

ITEM	Copyrights
DESCRIPTION	A copyright provides an owner with the exclusive rights to reproduce a work during the term of the copyright. The term of a copyright is the lifetime of the author plus 50 years. Copyrights are inexpensive to register.
WHERE TO OBTAIN	Copyright Office Library of Congress Washington, DC 20559 (202) 479-0700
COST	Call for forms and filing fee information.

ITEM	Inventor Information
DESCRIPTION	A source for inventors or innovators to obtain a commercial evaluation of their product or idea.
WHERE TO OBTAIN	Kansas Association of Inventors 2015 Lakin, Great Bend, KS 67530 (316) 792-1375
COST	Call for information.

ITEM	"Ideas Into Dollars"
DESCRIPTION	Publication provides information to aid the independent inventor and non-corporate innovator.
WHERE TO OBTAIN	U.S. Small Business Administration Publications P.O. Box 1000, Fort Worth, TX 76119 (800) 827-5722
COST	$2.00

ITEM	"Avoiding Patent, Trademark and Copyright Problems"
DESCRIPTION	Booklet provides a general overview of the steps that newcomers to a market need to take to avoid infringement. It may also encourage readers to look more closely at the value of protecting their own rights.
WHERE TO OBTAIN	Small Business Administration Publications, P.O. Box 1000 Fort Worth, TX 76119 (800) 827-5722
COST	$1.00

ITEM	"So You Have an Idea" "Copyright in Visual Arts" "Copyright for Computer Authors"
DESCRIPTION	Booklets providing general information for copyrighting.
WHERE TO OBTAIN	Innovation Clinic 2 White Street Concord, NH 03301
COST	$1.25 and a self-addressed, legal-sized envelope for each booklet.

No great deed is done
By falterers who ask for certainty.
... George Eliot

APPENDIX II
CHECKLIST INDEX

Business? It's quite simple: It's other
people's money.
... Alexandre Dumas

APPENDIX III
HOME BASED BUSINESSES

Operating a business from your home has a number of unique advantages. However, operating a home based business also can present some special problems. Refer to Chapter 8 which discusses keeping your home life and business life separate and to Chapter 14, which presents a number of suggestions on keeping your home based business looking "professional."

With a home based business you will also enjoy the following:

1. TAX SHELTER (tax deductions)

You should always obtain professional advice when it comes to taxes, but, in general, when operating a home based business you can tax deduct just about anything that is used for business purposes. In some cases, the law requires the item be used for business purposes for more than 50% of the time. Deductible items can include:

Home (see note)
Automobile
Interest on loans
Club memberships and books
Professional dues and subscriptions
Computer equipment and other supplies
Tools
Repairs
Utilities
Business travel
Education expenses

Note: You may deduct home-office expenses only if you use a portion of your home for the SOLE PURPOSE of your business and none other. The amount you may deduct is proportional to the space used for the business. Finally, you can't deduct an amount more than your business income.

One word of caution is that your business must be legitimate. You must be attempting to make a profit (i.e., your hobby cannot be a business). The IRS will generally assume you are trying if you show a profit in three out of five years. Keep detailed records to show your intentions and you may be able to continue to take deductions beyond this time limitation.

For more information on home based business deductions and what expenses may qualify, refer to Publication 587 (Business Use of Your Home) and Publication 334 (Tax Guide for Small Business), both of which are available from the IRS.

2. NO COMMUTING

If your business is a full time endeavor, you will be amazed at the extra time you have and the money you save by not having to commute daily to a "regular job."

3. INCREASED IRA BENEFITS

Immediately hire your spouse to work in the business. In this way, your spouse can have a separate IRA account allowing you up to a $2000 deduction yearly. This only works if your spouse is earning less than $10,000 from other sources.

To stay out of trouble with the IRS, ensure that your spouse is doing real work for the business and is being paid a reasonable wage. Some other advantages of having your spouse on the payroll include the following (check with your CPA or tax advisor for details):

- Ability to deduct 100% of your medical insurance premiums.

- Deduct spouse travel expenses.

- Reduce amount of "double taxation" if your business is a C-corporation by the amount of the spouse's wages.

4. DISCOUNT BUYING

Your business will be able to purchase just about everything at a discount ... from pens and paper to computers. You will find it is very easy to obtain "business" or "professional" discounts with nearly every supplier. These discounts can range up to 50% and can represent considerable savings over a year. And remember, much of what you purchase will be for both personal and business use.

Discount buying is simple. Seek out the wholesale and commercial outlets for whatever it is you need. Ask for a discount when making the purchase. Be prepared to present a purchase order (which you have previously purchased with your business name and address imprinted) and a business check. You need not ask for credit terms although some establishments will offer terms on the spot. In any case, always ask for the forms needed to open a credit account, fill them out and return them.

Every credit account you receive can be used to obtain others.

If possible, deal with other small business. Like you, they are always looking for a new customer and will be more inclined to work with you. It is more likely you will receive a discount from your local hardware store (as a business customer) than from a giant "discount" hardware chain.

5. BUSINESS TRAVEL

Travel that is business related is deductible as a business expense. Plan your vacations and other travel around business activities such as visiting potential customers or suppliers or attending business meetings. Check with your accountant for the details concerning this kind of deduction. You will find that for the most part a significant percentage of your vacation travel may be deductible.

APPENDIX IV
INTERNET INFORMATION

This appendix contains four sections:
1. Internet locations to "visit"
2. A Glossary of terms
3. References
4. Example of a World Wide Web Page

1. INTERNET LOCATIONS

The listing below provides a number of interesting and useful Internet addresses (or universal resource locators, URL's). Some of what follows will not have a lot of meaning until you become familiar with the Internet but rest assured that, when you start using the Internet for gathering information, these "resources" should prove helpful.

All the resources listed are most easily accessed using one of the popular World Wide Web browsers such as Netscape or Explorer. Ask your Internet provider for details on how to obtain browser software. Some are free.

The Internet is very large and growing at an amazing rate. Internet sites come and go quickly so be patient when browsing. Usually when a site moves or is discontinued some message is given to point you in another useful direction.

There are thousands of sites on the Internet and our listing is only a few of the sites of interest to the small business owner and entrepreneur. There are powerful internet search sites (called "engines") that allow you to find sites of interest based on your own search criteria. Just about anything ... and I mean anything ...you want information about is available on the Internet. For example, you could search on "business plans" or "biplanes" or "George Washington" or "metaphysics." A given search can return thousands of sites for you to investigate.

The listings below include the name of the site, its Internet address (URL), and in some cases, a brief description.

Have fun "surfing the net!"

---

http://www.isquare.com
The Small Business Advisor. An award-winning website dedicated to helping the new business owner be successful.

http://www.business.gov/
US Business Advisor

http://www.sbaonline.sba.gov/
The U.S. Small Business Administration. A major source of information for small businesses.

http://www.score.org
This site lists **SCORE** (Service Corps of Retired Executives) volunteers who you may E-mail for business advice and free small-business counseling.

http://www.law.vill.edu/Fed-Agency/fedwebloc.html
The Federal Web Locator

http://www-far.npr.gov/
Acquisition Reform Net. Lots of information relating to doing business with the U.S. Government

http://www.tollfree.att.net/dir800/
AT&T 800 Directory. An easy way to save a few dollars on your telephone bill.

http://telephonebook.com
Central Source **Yellow Pages**. Searchable by State and Country.

http://www.mediafinder.com
MediaFinder. A database of newsletters, magazines, journals, & catalogs by subject category.

http://www.inc.com/
Inc. Magazine. Archives, resources, references, discussion groups, etc ...

http://www.smalloffice.com
Your Small Office. From the editors of Small Business Computing and Home Office Computing Magazines.

http://www.counsel.com/qrfp/
Quick Request for Proposals. Free interactive directory service for business attorneys. Submit a brief description of a legal problem and get a proposal from a qualified attorney.

http://www.sbaer.uca.edu
Small Business Advancement National Center. A wide variety of information of interest to the small business owner and entrepreneur.

http://www.planware.ie/resource/planware
Planware. Advice on business plans, downloadable financial planners and other resources.

http://www.aaabiz.com/JG/ideasite.htm
Idea Site. An excellent source of small business marketing information.

http://www.corporate.com
Incorporating Guide. Up to date information to allow you to incorporate in any state easily and quickly.

http://www.primetimeps.com
Primetime PS Business Page. Information for self employed persons concerning advertising, incorporation, taxation, web etiquette and many other areas.

http://www.investoralert.com
The Investor Alert Resource Center

http://www.businessfinance.com/
Looking for business capital?

http://www.stroud.com
Stroud's Consummate Winsock Apps Page. A fantastic listing of Internet-related applications software with ratings & descriptions.

http://www.indo.com/distance/
How Far is it? Find the distance between any two locations in the United States.

http://www.netearnings.com
America's Small Business Financial Center

The following table lists a few of the largest search engines on the Internet today along with some others that allow you to search for specific information

http://www.lycos.com
Lycos. Good for general searching

http://www.hotbot.com
HotBot. Search the web, Usenet

http://www.excite.com
Excite. Search the web, Usenet news & classifieds

http://www.altavista.digital.com
AltaVista. Powerful for the web but not good for Usenet

http://www.infoseek.com
Infoseek. Good for basic searches. Full-text index of all pages

http://www.dejanews.com
Deja News. The ultimate newsgroup search engine

http://www.metacrawler.com
Metacrawler. Meta search site using 9 engines including Lycos,Excite,Open Text,Webcrawler

http://www.m-w.com/netdict.htm
Dictionary by Webster. Search for a word or phrase.

http://www.columbia.edu/acis/bartleby/bartlett/
Bartlett's familiar quotations. Search is available which will list every quotation containing a selected word(s).

http://www.thesaurus.com/
Roget's Thesarus. Handier and faster than the "real thing."

http://www.almanac.com/
The Old Farmers Almanac. No kidding. It even LOOKS like the almanac.

http://www.refdesk.com/
My Virtual Reference Desk
An amazing amount of information. Check it out - there is too much to list here.

2. GLOSSARY OF INTERNET TERMS

ADDRESS. A location of a specific site on the Internet. It can be either numeric or alphanumeric. For example, the address of Yahoo, a very powerful search-engine is "http://www.yahoo.com.

BBS. Bulletin Board System. A menu driven computer interface accessible via modem. A BBS can be accessed directly or via the Internet.

BROWSER. Software that is used to display WWW Internet pages for viewing.

COMM SOFTWARE. COMMunications software is required to allow your personal computer to connect via modem to the outside world. These programs are inexpensive and easy to use.

DOMAIN NAME SYSTEM. An addressing system that is used to describe specific sites on the Internet. Address elements are separated by periods (.) and go from the specific to the general.

DOWNLOAD. Retrieving a file from a remote computer or host.

FAQ. (Frequently Asked Questions). A listing that allows a new user to a newsgroup to find answers to commonly asked questions.

FTP. (File Transfer Protocol). This is the protocol (computers talk to one another using a "protocol") utilized to transfer files on the Internet.

GOPHER. A popular application used to find and retrieve files from the Internet.

HOST. This is a computer tied directly into the Internet. An example would be the computer that you dial into at your Internet provider.

HYPERTEXT. This is a system in which certain (usually underlined) words actually represent "links" to other places within the text or to other Internet locations. This is the basis for powerful information retrieval.

NETIQUETTE. Internet etiquette.

NETSCAPE. A popular WWW browser.

NEWSGROUP. A Usenet discussion group. There are presently over 12,000 of these groups.

PPP. (Point-to-Point Protocol). This is the method of transferring information to the Internet via a telephone line.

PROTOCOL. Computers talk to one another using a specific series of commands called a protocol.

SHAREWARE. Software that may be downloaded from various sites on the Internet. Payment is on the honor system.

SIGNATURE. A short note at the end of E-mail or other messages that usually contains your name, address, and other brief information.

TCP/IP. (Transmission Control Protocol/Internet Protocol). This is a special protocol that determines how data is transmitted on the Internet. It ensures that data gets to where it's addressed.

TELNET. An Internet protocol that will allow you to log into a remote computer on the net.

URL. (Universal Resource Locator). This specifies a certain location on the WWW.

VERONICA. A system on the Internet that allows you to search Gopher menus.

WWW. (World Wide Web). A very powerful system that utilizes hypertext to allow linking from within a document to another document somewhere else on the net. The WWW is the fastest growing service of the Internet and contains thousands of sites. The WWW is most conveniently accessed with a browser such as Netscape.

3. REFERENCES

The following material is available at most libraries and book stores. Prices shown are approximate.

"Internet for Dummies" by Levine & Baroudi, 1994. $20. (A good primer)

"More Internet for Dummies" by Levine & Young, 1994. $20. (Read this one after you have read the previous reference)

"The Whole Internet" by Krol. $25. (A good listing of Internet providers and resources)

"Internet Secrets" by Levine & Baroudi. $40. (A BIG book with lots of information)

"Using the Internet" by Que books. 2nd ed. $40.

"The Internet Yellow Pages" by Hahn & Stout, 1995, 2nd ed. $30. (Contains thousands of Internet sites arranged in the typical yellow-pages format. A great reference and remember that the Internet is growing so fast that any reference listing such as this will be quickly out of date)

"The Internet Guide for New Users" by Daniel Dern. $28. (A good choice for the beginner. Contains a good index and glossary)

"Making Money on the Internet" by Alfred and Emily Glossbrenner. $20. (Easy reading)

"The Internet Business Book" by Jill and Matthew Ellsworth. $23. (My choice for the business owner who is interested in the Internet)

"Online Marketing Handbook" by Daniel Janal.

"The Internet Business Companion: Growing Your Business in the Electronic Age," by Angell and Heslop, 1994. $20.

4. EXAMPLE OF A WORLD WIDE WEB PAGE

An example of a World Wide Web page is shown on the next page.

APPENDIX V
OBTAINING A MERCHANT
CARD ACCOUNT

There is little doubt as to the value of being able to take credit cards as payment for your product or service. This merchant status requires you to deal with a provider or electronic clearing house for the credit card transactions and a participating bank for deposit of your funds. The process simply involves finding a bank that will accept you as a merchant card customer.

The problem is that it can be difficult to obtain a merchant account if you do not have a store front operation or if the majority of your business is via mail order. Currently, most banks are simply not interested in working with you unless you are a "traditional" business owner. However, with the proliferation of mail order and home based businesses, many electronic clearing houses are associated with banks that cater to the mail order business. That's the good news. The bad news is that if you are not very careful, your merchant account will cost you a lot more than necessary.

This appendix provides information to assist you in evaluating various banks and ensure you are getting the best deal possible. You do not need one of the numerous "manuals" that sell for up to $60 and claim to "guide you through the process." The "process" is actually very simple ... you just need to find the best deal out there by using the information provided here.

Finding a provider.

First, try going to your own bank and ask if they will help. If they will, be sure and review the various charges discussed below. Be careful since many banks deal with agents who in turn represent an electronic clearing house. These agents are commissioned and are not looking out for your interests. If your bank won't help, check the yellow pages under "Credit Card & Other Credit Plans-Equipment & Supplies" or similar heading. You may also search the Internet which is how we found our merchant account provider. Most listings will be agents that represent an electronic clearing house or the clearing houses themselves. Remember, talk only to the electronic clearing houses. It may not be clear if you're talking with a clearing house or an agent, so ask!

Transaction costs.

There is a discount rate (expressed as a percentage of the sale) associated with each credit card transaction. This rate is always higher for mail order businesses, but you should not pay much over 2%. A transaction fee is also charged and this should be approximately 20-cents.

Hardware/software requirements.

You will need a terminal (or software) which allows you to enter credit card data and obtain authorization for each charge. The terminal connects to a telephone line and calls the clearing house; with software you need a computer and modem. This is an area where many providers make their money. Terminal costs can range from $300 to $2000 (the terminals are all basically the same). Software, usually by "IC Verify," is approximately $350. Many providers require that you purchase or lease equipment from them and will tell you cost is not negotiable. This is not necessarily true. One provider told us their terminal was priced at $1200. Later they reduced the cost to $800. Finally they agreed to $400. You should not pay more than $375 for a terminal. In addition to the terminal you might want a printer to generate a "sales receipt" for the customer which you will mail with the merchandise or invoice. Typical printer costs are $150-250. You do not need a printer, however, since you can use a manual imprinter (usually furnished free) for receipts.

I recommend you purchase software. It's handier and no additional printer is required since you can use your computer system printer. Furthermore, there are no hassles with warranties, electronic failures and mechanical problems. Do not deal with a provider if they will not allow software as an alternate to a terminal.

Questions (Q) and Comments (C).

Questions to ask the perspective provider before committing. Each question is followed by a comment to assist you in determining a "satisfactory" answer.

Q: *Are there any application fees?*

C: There should be none although some providers charge up to $500.

Q: Are there any installation or programming fees?

C: There should be none although some providers charge up to $100.

Q: Are there any statement fees?

C: There should be none, although some banks charge a monthly statement fee of up to $15/month.

Q: Is there a minimum account billing?

C: There should be none, although some banks charge a monthly fee of up to $50 for accounts that do not meet the minimum.

Q: Is there a chargeback fee?

C: A chargeback occurs when a bankcard customer has their account credited for a prior purchase (i.e., merchandise returned under a guarantee). There should be no fees to you for this although some providers charge up to $10.

Q: Is there a voice authorization fee?

C: A voice authorization is required when your terminal or software is not available. The provider usually has a toll-free number to use for this purpose. There should be no charge but some will charge up to $1/call.

Q: What are the transaction fees?

C: These fees are in addition to the discount rate charge on each transaction. They can vary depending on the form of the transaction and, in general, bankcard numbers taken over the telephone are slightly more expensive. A fair fee is 20-cents per transaction.

Q: Is there a bank setup fee?

C: This is typical of a fee you will not find out about until the 11th hour unless you ask. There should be no setup fee but some banks charge up to $50.

Q: Is there a daily close-out fee?

C: You will normally "close-out" your transactions at the end of each business day. This is done by a simple transmittal to the provider via your software or terminal. There should be no fees associated with this.

Q: When is customer support available?

C: Support should be available to you via a toll-free number during normal business hours.

Q: Is a reserve account required?

C: Some banks will require that you maintain a reserve account whose amount is determined by your estimated sales receipts. You should not deal with a bank that requires this reserve.

Q: When will funds be available?

C: That is, what is the time delay between a transaction and when the money is available in the bank? It should not be longer than 3-days.

Q: *Is money deposited in my own local bank?*

C: In some cases, the provider's bank will require that funds be placed in their bank, and not yours. If this is the case, you simply move funds from their bank to yours a few times a month.

Q: *What is the equipment warranty and what assistance is available if the terminal becomes defective?*

C: Warranty should be at least a year and if you are leasing, as long as the lease. A 'loaner' should be available if your terminal requires repair. (Note: We strongly recommend you do not lease. We didn't find a single supplier who had lease terms that were acceptable.)

Q: *What credit cards can be processed?*

C: Visa and Mastercard are usually processed. You can easily add Discover at no cost but there are additional fees associated with American Express.

Q: *Is a manual imprinter available?*

C: This should be included at no charge.

All the fees are negotiable. As a mail order business you may not have much clout with which to bargain, but the right provider will charge few, if any of these fees. The only charges you should incur are the normal transaction fees and cost of equipment or software.

Recommendation

When shopping for a merchant account we were turned down by our own local bank of over 15 years. We searched and talked to a LOT of providers, many of whom had no interest whatsoever in dealing with a mail order or home-based business and others who had a variety of outrageous fees associated with the account. Our research finally led us to an electronic clearing house who had no problems with mail order and home-based businesses and who had virtually no fees! They are out there ... you just need to search them out.

For a point of reference, we paid approximately $350 for the software (which was our preferred approach) and a discount rate (for a manual entry; i.e., mail order) of 2.00% with a 20-cent transaction fee. If the credit card is "swiped;" i.e., you have the credit card in hand and can pass it through a reader, the discount rate drops to 1.75%. The only fee is a $10 statement fee and $20 fee if sales are less than $1,000/month.

APPENDIX VI
GLOSSARY

ACCOUNTING PERIOD

A period of time, (month, quarter, year), for which a financial statement is produced.

ACCOUNTS PAYABLE

This represents what a business owes to its suppliers and other creditors at a given point in time.

ACCOUNTS RECEIVABLE

This represents the amount due to a business by its customers at a given point in time.

ACCRUAL ACCOUNTING

A method of bookkeeping in which income and expenses are allocated to periods to which they apply, regardless of when actually received or paid. For example, when an invoice is rendered, its value is added to income immediately, even though it has not been paid. (Also see CASH ACCOUNTING)

AUDIT

Verification of financial records and accounting procedures generally conducted by a CPA or accounting firm or if you're really unlucky, the IRS.

BALANCE SHEET

Financial statement showing assets and liabilities at a specific time.

BOND

A third party obligation promising to pay if a vendor does not fulfill its valid obligations under a contract. Types of bonds include LICENSE, PERFORMANCE, BID, INDEMNITY & PAYMENT. (Also see SURETY BOND)

BREAK-EVEN POINT

The point at which sales equal total costs.

CAPITAL ASSET

An asset that is purchased for long-term use such as machinery and equipment.

CASH ACCOUNTING

The simplest form of accounting in which income is considered earned when received and expenses are not taken into account until paid.

CAVEAT EMPTOR

"Let the buyer beware"

CERTIFIED LENDERS

Banks that participate in the SBA's guaranteed loan program.

COLLATERAL

An asset that can be sold for cash and which has been pledged to a creditor to secure a future obligation. (For example, if you finance a car it is the collateral for the loan).

COMPOUND INTEREST

Interest earned on previously accumulated interest plus the original principal. Most spread sheets can calculate this easily for you but for the curious, the formula is $C = P(1 + r/n)n$, where C=compound amount, P=original principal, r=annual interest rate, n=total number of periods over which interest is compounded.

CONTRACT

An agreement between two (or more) parties in which each promises to perform in some way. Contracts can be complex and should always be reviewed by an attorney. A contract may not be binding if not correctly drafted and executed.

CREDIT REPORT

A listing of an individual or company's history of repaying past loans and other liabilities.

DEBT FINANCING

This is financing in which you get a loan from someone or somewhere and go into debt! You are obligated to repay the money at some pre-determined interest rate.

DEPRECIATION

Decrease in the value of equipment over time. Depreciation of equipment used for business is a tax-deductible expense.

DIRECT COSTS

Costs that are directly related to the manufacture of goods or of services such as labor cost (salaries) and materials. (Also see INDIRECT COSTS)

DROP SHIPMENT

A shipment directly from the manufacturer to the end user.

DUNS (Data Universal Numbering System)

A database maintained by Dun and Bradstreet that is used by the Government to identify each contractor and their location(s). This number is required to register with the Central Contractor Register (CCR) that is used by the government's electronic commerce/electronic data interchange (EC/EDI) system called FACNET. You can obtain a DUNS number at no cost by calling Dun and Bradstreet at (800) 333-0505.

EMPLOYER IDENTIFICATION NUMBER (EIN)

A number obtained by a business from the IRS by filing form SS-4. If you are a sole proprietorship, your EIN is your social security number.

ENTREPRENEUR

Someone who is willing to assume the responsibility, risk and rewards of starting and operating a business.

EQUITY FINANCING

This involves "selling" a portion of your company to an outside investor. You have no obligation to repay the funds. In general, venture capital firms provide this type of funding.

ESCROW

Temporary monetary deposit with an independent third party by agreement between two parties. The escrow money is released when certain agreed conditions have been met.

ESOP

(Employee Stock Ownership Plan). A plan where employees have a vested interest (stock ownership) in the company

FACTORING

The buying and selling of invoices or accounts receivables.

FIDUCIARY

A person or company entrusted with assets owned by another party (beneficiary), and responsible for investing the assets until they are turned over to the beneficiary.

FISCAL YEAR

Any 12-month period used by a company or government as an accounting period.

FIXED COST

A production cost which does not vary significantly with the volume of output. An example would be administrative costs. (Also see VARIABLE COST).

FRANCHISE

A franchise is a form of licensing. The franchiser provides his services through a series of franchisees. Before investing in any franchise, check with the International Franchise Association at 1 (800) 543-1038 to see if the franchise is a member in good standing.

FREE ON BOARD (FOB)

Commercial term in which the seller's obligations are fulfilled when the goods reach a point specified in the contract.

GRACE PERIOD

Time allowed a debtor in which legal action will not be undertaken by the creditor when payment is late.

GUARANTEE

Pledge by a third party to repay a loan in the event that the borrower cannot. A special case is a PERSONAL guarantee in which you personally guarantee an obligation.

GUARANTEED/INSURED LOANS

Programs in which the federal government makes an arrangement to indemnify a lender against part or all of any defaults by those responsible for repayment of loans. An example is a small business loan guaranteed by the SBA.

INDEMNITY

Obligation of one party to reimburse another party for losses which have occurred or which may occur.

INDIRECT COSTS

Costs that cannot be directly allocated to the manufacture of a specific product such as clerical salaries (Also see DIRECT COSTS).

JOB SHARING

Arrangement in which the responsibilities and hours of one job position are carried out by two people.

LETTER OF CREDIT

A bank instrument authorizing a seller to receive funds when certain conditions have been met (such as actual shipment of goods).

LIEN

Legal right to hold property of another party or to have it sold or applied in payment of a claim.

LIQUIDATION

Sale of the assets of a business to pay off debts.

MARGINAL COST

Additional cost associated with producing one more unit of output.

MINORITY BUSINESSES

The Small Business Administration defines minorities as those who are "socially and economically disadvantaged." The U.S. Code of Federal Regulations (CFR) contains the specific requirements.

OSDBU (Office of Small & Disadvantaged Business Utilization)

These offices offer small business information on procurement opportunities, guidance on procurement procedures, and identification of both prime and subcontracting opportunities with the United States Government.

OVERHEAD

Business expenses not directly related to a particular good or service produced. An example would be utilities.

PASS

This is the Procurement Automated Source System managed by the Small Business Administration. Registering with this central referral system of small businesses interested in selling to the government can bring you business with almost no effort. Registration is free. Call 1 (800) 231-7277.

POWER OF ATTORNEY

An agreement authorizing someone (generally an attorney) to act as your agent. This agreement may be general (complete authority) or special (limited authority).

PREFERRED LENDERS

Banks which have a special written agreement with the SBA which allows them to make a guaranteed SBA loan without prior SBA approval.

PROMPT PAYMENT ACT

A federal law that requires federal agencies to pay interest to companies on bills not paid within 30 days of invoice or completion of work.

SBC (Small Business Centers)

These 12 GSA centers located throughout the United States can help you tap the multi-billion-dollar GSA "market" for goods and services. Contact a center nearest you.

SBDC

Small Business Development Centers are located throughout the United States and are administered by the SBA. They provide management assistance to entrepreneurs and new business owners.

SBIC (Small Business Investment Corporation)

SBICs are licensed by the SBA as federally funded private venture capital firms. Money is available to small businesses under a variety of agreements.

SCORE

The Service Corps of Retired Executives is a volunteer management assistance program of the SBA. SCORE volunteers provide one-on-one counseling and workshops and seminars for small businesses. There are hundreds of SCORE offices throughout the United States.

SIC (Standard Industrial Classification Code)

A four-digit number assigned to identify a business based on the type of business or trade involved. The first two digits correspond to major groups such as construction and manufacturing, while the last two digits correspond to subgroups such as constructing homes versus constructing highways. A business can determine its SIC number by looking it up in a directory published by the Department of Commerce, or by checking in the SIC book in the reference section of a local library. SBA size standards are based on SIC codes.

SIMPLE INTEREST

Interest paid only on the principal of a loan.

SOLE PROPRIETORSHIP

The simplest (and most popular) form of business organization. The individual is personally liable for all debts of the business to the full extent of his or her property. On the other hand, the owner has complete control of the business.

SURETY BONDS

Surety bonds provide reimbursement to an individual, company or the government if a firm fails to complete a contract. SBA guarantees surety bonds in a program much like SBA's guaranteed loan program.

SWEAT EQUITY

A common form of "investment." This refers to the investment in time owners make, with no salary, to a new business.

TAX NUMBER

A number assigned to a business that enables the business to buy wholesale without paying sales tax on goods and products. Contact your local court house for additional information.

VARIABLE COST

Any costs which change significantly with the level of output. The obvious example is cost of materials.

VENTURE CAPITAL

Money used to support new or unusual undertakings; equity, risk or speculative investment capital. This funding is provided to new or existing firms which exhibit potential for above-average growth.

APPENDIX VII
STATE SPECIFIC INFORMATION

This appendix provides small business related points of contact for each state. We've done our best to provide correct telephone numbers but it's hard to keep current. Up to date information is generally available on the state's Internet website.

For additional state information, the SBA publishes "The States and Small Business: A Directory of Programs and Activities." Although slightly out of date (1993) it contains a great deal of information. Cost $21.00 from the Government Printing Office at (202) 512-1800. Order #045-000-00266-7.

GENERAL NOTES FOR ALL ENTRIES

1. OSHA. The Occupational Safety & Health Administration offices oversee compliance with federal safety guidelines.

2. POSTAL BUSINESS CENTERS provide assistance to small businesses in making their mail automation-compatible and thus reducing costs. There may be more than one center in your state. Call the number shown in the table and ask for the location nearest you.

3. U.S. DEPT OF COMMERCE DISTRICT OFFICES provide information on international markets and exporting.

4. SBA DISTRICT OFFICES provide a wide variety of small business assistance. The SBA can be reached at (800) 827-5722.

5. STATE CHAMBER OF COMMERCE can provide business-related information for specific areas of the state and how to get involved in local chambers. This is a great way to market via networking.

6. FINANCIAL ASSISTANCE offices provide information on loans, grants, and venture capital.

7. PROCUREMENT ASSISTANCE offices assist small businesses in marketing to the state and local governments.

8. SBDC (Small Business Development Centers) provide a wide-range of assistance for new businesses. The number given is for the "lead" SBDC in your state. Ask for the location/number of the center nearest you.

9. PUBLICATIONS numbers are points of contact for obtaining state-specific small business assistance guides and booklets.

10. Prefix "http://" to all website addresses.

ALABAMA

Website Address	www.ado.state.al.us
Business Development	(334) 242-0400
Dep't of Commerce Office	(205) 731-1331
Financial Assistance	(334) 223-7008
Incorporation Information	(205) 242 5324
Minority Opportunities	(334) 242-2220
OSHA	(205) 441-6131
Postal Business Center	(205) 521-0364
Procurement Assistance	(205) 934-7260
SBA District Office	(205) 731-1344
SBDC	(205) 934-7260

ALASKA

Website Address	www.state.ak.us
Business Development	(907) 465-2017
Chamber of Commerce	(907) 586-2323
Dep't of Commerce Office	(907) 271-6237
Financial Assistance	(907) 465-2510
Incorporation Information	(907) 465-2530
Minority Opportunities	(907) 562-0335
OSHA	(907) 269-4939
Postal Business Center	(907) 564-2823
SBA District Office	(907) 271-4022
SBDC	(907) 274-7232

ARIZONA

Website Address	www.state.az.us
Business Development	(800) 264-3377
Dep't of Commerce Office	(602) 640-2513
Financial Assistance	(602) 280-1352
Incorporation Information	(602) 542-4285
OSHA	(602) 542-5795
Postal Business Center	(602) 223-3535
SBA District Office	(602) 640-2316
SBDC	(602) 731-8720
Small Biz Publications	(602) 280-1480

ARKANSAS

Website Address	www.state.ar.us
Business Development	(501) 682-1121
Dep't of Commerce Office	(501) 324-5794
Financial Assistance	(501) 374-9247
Incorporation Information	(501) 682-3409
Minority Opportunities	(501) 682-1060
OSHA	(501) 682-4526
Postal Business Center	(501) 521-0364
Procurement Assistance	(501) 324-9312
Publications	(501) 324-9043
SBA District Office	(501) 324-5871
SBDC	(501) 324-9043

CALIFORNIA

Website Address	www.state.ca.us
Business Development	(916) 324-1295
Dep't of Commerce Office	(310) 235-7104
Financial Assistance	(916) 324-1295
Incorporation Information	(916) 445-0620
Minority Opportunities	(916) 322-5060
OSHA (Federal)	(916) 975-4310
Postal Business Center	(415) 536-6565
SBA District Office	(916) 744-2118
SBDC	(916) 324-5068
Small Business Help Line	(916) 327-4357

COLORADO

Website Address	www.state.co.us
Business Development	(303) 892-3840
Dep't of Commerce Office	(303) 844-6622
Financial Assistance	(303) 892-3840
Incorporation Information	(303) 894-2200
Minority Opportunities	(303) 892-3840
OSHA (State)	(970) 491-6151
Postal Business Center	(303) 297-6118
SBA District Office	(303) 844-3984
SBDC	(303) 892-3809
Small Biz Publications	(303) 582-5920

CONNECTICUT

Website Address	www..state.ct.us
Business Development	(860) 258-4200
Dep't of Commerce Office	(860) 638-6950
Financial Assistance	(800) 392-2122
Incorporation Information	(203) 566-8827
Minority Opportunities	(800) 392-2122
OSHA (State)	(860) 566-4550
Postal Business Center	(860) 610-3108
SBA District Office	(860) 240-4700
SBDC	(860) 486-4135

DELAWARE

Website Address	www.state.de.us
Business Development	(302) 739-4271
Chamber of Commerce	(302) 655-7221
Dep't of Commerce Office	(215) 597-6101
Financial Assistance	(302) 739-4271
Incorporation Information	(302) 739-3073
OSHA	(302) 761-8200
Postal Business Center	(302) 323-3733
Publications	(302) 739-4271
SBA District Office	(302) 573-6294
SBDC	(302) 831-1555

DISTRICT of COLUMBIA

Website Address	www.ci. washington.dc.us
Business Development	(202) 727-6365
Chamber of Commerce	(202) 638-3222
Dep't of Commerce Office	(804) 771-2246
Financial Assistance	(202) 535-1942
Incorporation Information	(202) 727-7278
Minority Opportunities	(202) 724-1385
OSHA	(202) 576-6339
Postal Business Center	(301) 565-2177
SBA District Office	(202) 606-4000
SBDC	(202) 806-1550

FLORIDA

Website Address	www.state.fl.us
Business Development	(407) 316-4600
Chamber of Commerce	(904) 425-1200
Dep't of Commerce Office	(813) 461-0011
Financial Assistance	(407) 316-4646
Incorporation Information	(904) 488-3680
OSHA	(904) 488-3044
Postal Business Center	(305) 470-0803
Publications	(407) 316-4600
SBA District Office	(305) 536-5521
SBDC	(904) 444-2060

GEORGIA

Website Address	www.gditt.com
Business Development	(404) 656-3545
Chamber of Commerce	(404) 223-2264
Dep't of Commerce Office	(404) 657-1900
Financial Assistance	(404) 656-3556
Incorporation Information	(404) 656-2881
Minority Opportunities	(404) 656-6315
OSHA	(404) 894-2646
Postal Business Center	(912) 752-8717
Procurement Assistance	(404) 542-5760
SBA District Office	(404) 347-2441
SBDC	(706) 542-6762

HAWAII

Website Address	www.state.hi.us
Business Development	(808) 586-2591
Chamber of Commerce	(808) 545-4300
Dep't of Commerce Office	(808) 541-1782
Financial Assistance	(808) 586-2576
Incorporation Information	(808) 586-2820
Minority Opportunities	(808) 433-6394
OSHA	(808) 586-9116
Postal Business Center	(808) 423-3761
Procurement Assistance	(808) 586-2591
Publications	(808) 586-2600
SBA District Office	(808) 541-2990
SBDC	(808) 933-3515

IDAHO

Website Address	www.state.id.us
Business Development	(208) 334-2470
Dep't of Commerce Office	(208) 334-2470
Financial Assistance	(208) 772-0584
Incorporation Information	(208) 334-2300
Minority Opportunities	(208) 344-2531
OSHA	(208) 385-3283
Publications	(208) 334-2470
SBA District Office	(208) 334-1696
SBDC	(208) 385-1640

ILLINOIS

Website Address	www.state.il.us
Business Development	(800) 252-2923
Chamber of Commerce	(312) 983-7100
Dep't of Commerce Office	(312) 353-8040
Financial Assistance	(312) 814-2308
Incorporation Information	(217) 785-3285
Minority Opportunities	(312) 814-3540
OSHA	(312) 488-3044
Postal Business Center	(305) 814-2337
Procurement Assistance	(217) 524-0160
SBA District Office	(305) 353-4528
SBDC	(217) 524-5856

INDIANA

Website Address	www.state.in.us
Business Development	(317) 232-8800
Chamber of Commerce	(317) 264-3110
Dep't of Commerce Office	(317) 582-2300
Financial Assistance	(317) 233-4332
Incorporation Information	(317) 232-6587
Minority Opportunities	(317) 264-2820
OSHA	(317) 226-7290
Postal Business Center	(317) 464-6010
Procurement Assistance	(317) 233-3901
SBA District Office	(317) 226-7272
SBDC	(317) 264-6871

IOWA

Website Address	www.state.ia.us
Business Development	(515) 242-4707
Dep't of Commerce Office	(515) 284-4222
Financial Assistance	(515) 242-4831
Incorporation Information	(515) 281-7550
Minority Opportunities	(515) 242-4948
OSHA	(515) 281-3606
Postal Business Center	(515) 251-2336
Procurement Assistance	(515) 242-4949
SBA District Office	(515) 284-4222
SBDC	(515) 292-6351

KANSAS

Website Address	www.state.ks.us
Business Development	(913) 296-3481
Chamber of Commerce	(913) 357-6616
Dep't of Commerce Office	(913) 269-6160
Financial Assistance	(913) 296-2652
Incorporation Information	(913) 296-2236
OSHA	(913) 296-4386
Postal Business Center	(316) 946-4528
Procurement Assistance	(913) 296-5298
Minority Opportunities	(913) 296-5298
SBA District Office	(316) 269-6273
SBDC	(316) 689-3193

KENTUCKY

Website Address	www.state.ky.us
Business Development	(502) 564-4252
Chamber of Commerce	(502) 695-4700
Dep't of Commerce Office	(502) 582-5066
Financial Assistance	(502) 564-4554
Incorporation Information	(502) 564-2848
OSHA	(502) 564-6895
Postal Business Center	(502) 473-4200
Procurement Assistance	(502) 564-4252
Minority Opportunities	(502) 564-2064
SBA District Office	(502) 582-5971
SBDC	(606) 257-7668

LOUISIANA

Website Address	www.state.la.us
Business Development	(504) 342-5893
Minority Opportunities	(504) 342-5373
Dep't of Commerce Office	(504) 589-6546
Financial Assistance	(504) 342-5398
Incorporation Information	(504) 925-4716
OSHA	(504) 389-0474
Postal Business Center	(504) 589-1366
Publications	(504) 342-5893
SBA District Office	(504) 589-2354
SBDC	(318) 342-5506

MAINE

Website Address	www.state.me.us
Business Development	(207) 287-3153
Chamber of Commerce	(207) 623-4568
Dep't of Commerce Office	(617) 424-5950
Financial Assistance	(207) 623-3263
Incorporation Information	(207) 289-4195
OSHA	(207) 624-6460
Postal Business Center	(207) 871-8567
Publications	(800) 541-5872
SBA District Office	(207) 622-8378
SBDC	(207) 780-4420

MARYLAND

Website Address	www.state.md.us
Business Development	(410) 767-6300
Chamber of Commerce	(410) 269-0642
Dep't of Commerce Office	(410) 962-4539
Financial Assistance	(410) 767-7850
Incorporation Information	(410) 767-1340
Minority Opportunities	(410) 767-8232
OSHA	(410) 333-4100
Postal Business Center	(410) 347-4358
SBA District Office	(410) 962-4392
SBDC	(410) 767-6552

MASSACHUSETTS

Website Address	www.state.ma.us
Business Development	(617) 727-3206
Chamber of Commerce	(617) 894-4700
Dep't of Commerce Office	(617) 424-5990
Financial Assistance	(617) 451-2477
Minority Opportunities	(617) 727-8692
Incorporation Information	(617) 727-2853
OSHA	(617) 727-3982
Postal Business Center	(617) 938-1450
Publications	(617) 727-2834
SBA District Office	(617) 565-5590
SBDC	(413) 545-6301

MICHIGAN

Website Address	www.state.mi.us
Business Development	(517) 373-9808
Chamber of Commerce	(517) 371-2100
Dep't of Commerce Office	(517) 226-3650
Financial Assistance	(517) 373-9808
Incorporation Information	(517) 334-6327
OSHA	(517) 322-1831
Postal Business Center	(313) 226-8600
Procurement Assistance	(313) 373-9808
Minority Opportunities	(517) 373-9808
SBA District Office	(517) 536-5521
SBDC	(313) 964-1798

MINNESOTA

Website Address	www.state.mn.us
Business Development	(612) 282-2103
Chamber of Commerce	(612) 292-4650
Dep't of Commerce Office	(612) 348-1638
Financial Assistance	(612) 297-1391
Incorporation Information	(612) 296-9215
OSHA	(612) 296-2116
Postal Business Center	(612) 349-6360
Procurement Assistance	(612) 296-2600
Publications	(612) 296-3871
SBA District Office	(612) 370-2324
SBDC	(612) 297-5770

MISSISSIPPI

Website Address	www.state.ms.us
Business Development	(601) 359-3449
Dep't of Commerce Office	(601) 965-4388
Financial Assistance	(601) 359-3552
Incorporation Information	(601) 359-1350
Minority Opportunities	(601) 362-2260
OSHA	(601) 987-3981
Postal Business Center	(601) 351-7100
Procurement Assistance	(601) 864-2961
SBA District Office	(601) 965-4378
SBDC	(601) 232-5001

MISSOURI

Website Address	www.state.mo.us
Business Development	(573) 751-9045
Chamber of Commerce	(573) 634-3511
Dep't of Commerce Office	(816) 426-3141
Financial Assistance	(573) 751-0717
Incorporation Information	(573) 751-4194
OSHA	(573) 751-3403
Postal Business Center	(314) 534-2678
Minority Opportunities	(573) 751-3237
SBA District Office	(816) 374-6708
SBDC	(573) 882-0344

MONTANA

Website Address	www.state.mt.us
Business Development	(406) 444-3494
Chamber of Commerce	(406) 442-2405
Dep't of Commerce Office	(406) 844-6622
Financial Assistance	(406) 444-4187
Incorporation Information	(406) 444-3665
Minority Opportunities	(406) 444-6337
OSHA	(406) 444-6401
Procurement Assistance	(406) 444-6337
Postal Business Center	(406) 255-6432
Publications	(406) 444-3814
SBA District Office	(406) 441-1081
SBDC	(406) 444-4780

NEBRASKA

Website Address	www.state.ne.us
Business Development	(402) 471-3782
Chamber of Commerce	(402) 474-4422
Dep't of Commerce Office	(402) 221-3664
Financial Assistance	(402) 434-3900
Incorporation Information	(402) 471-4079
Minority Opportunities	(402) 221-3604
OSHA	(402) 471-4717
Postal Business Center	(402) 573-2100
SBA District Office	(402) 221-4691
SBDC	(402) 554-2521

NEVADA

Website Address	www.state.nv.us
Business Development	(702) 486-4335
Chamber of Commerce	(702) 686-3030
Dep't of Commerce Office	(702) 784-5203
Financial Assistance	(702) 687-4250
Incorporation Information	(702) 687-5203
Minority Opportunities	(702) 486-4335
OSHA	(702) 486-5020
Postal Business Center	(702) 361-9318
Procurement Assistance	(702) 687-4325
SBA District Office	(702) 388-6611
SBDC	(702) 784-1717

NEW HAMSHIRE

Website Address	www.state.nh.us
Business Development	(603) 271-2591
Dep't of Commerce Office	(617) 424-5990
Financial Assistance	(603) 271-2391
Incorporation Information	(603) 271-3244
OSHA	(603) 271-2024
Postal Business Center	(603) 644-3838
Procurement Assistance	(603) 271-2591
Publications	(603) 271-2591
SBA District Office	(603) 225-1400
SBDC	(603) 862-2200

NEW JERSEY

Website Address	www.state.nj.us
Business Development	(609) 292-3860
Chamber of Commerce	(609) 989-7888
Dep't of Commerce Office	(609) 989-2100
Financial Assistance	(609) 292-1800
Incorporation Information	(609) 984-1900
Minority Opportunities	(609) 292-3860
OSHA	(609) 292-3923
Postal Business Center	(201) 468-7064
Publications	(609) 292-3860
SBA District Office	(609) 645-2434
SBDC	(201) 648-5950

NEW MEXICO

Website Address	www.state.nm.us
Business Development	(505) 827-0300
Dep't of Commerce Office	(505) 827-0350
Financial Assistance	(505) 827-0300
Incorporation Information	(505) 827-3616
Minority Opportunities	(505) 841-8920
OSHA	(505) 827-4231
Postal Business Center	(505) 245-9480
Procurement Assistance	(505) 827-0425
Publications	(505) 438-1362
SBA District Office	(305) 766-1870
SBDC	(505) 438-1362

NEW YORK

Website Address	www.state.ny.us
Business Development	(518) 473-0499
Dep't of Commerce Office	(716) 551-4191
Financial Assistance	(518) 473-9741
Incorporation Information	(518) 474-6200
Minority Opportunities	(212) 803-2411
OSHA	(518) 457-2072
Postal Business Center	(518) 464-7475
Procurement Assistance	(518) 474-7756
SBA District Office	(716) 551-4301
SBDC	(518) 443-5398

NORTH CAROLINA

Website Address	www.state.nc.us
Business Development	(919) 715-7272
Dep't of Commerce Office	(910) 333-5345
Financial Assistance	(919) 571-4154
Incorporation Information	(919) 733-4161
OSHA	(919) 856-4770
Postal Business Center	(919) 420-5165
Procurement Assistance	(919) 733-8965
SBA District Office	(704) 344-6563
SBDC	(919) 571-4154

NORTH DAKOTA

Website Address	www.state.nd.us
Business Development	(701) 857-3825
Chamber of Commerce	(701) 222-0929
Dep't of Commerce Office	(402) 221-3664
Financial Assistance	(701) 328-5300
Incorporation Information	(701) 224-2900
OSHA	(701) 328-5188
Minority Opportunities	(701) 328-5300
Publications	(701) 777-3132
SBA District Office	(701) 239-5131
SBDC	(701) 777-3700

OHIO

Website Address	www.state.oh.us
Business Development	(614) 466-4232
Chamber of Commerce	(614) 228-4201
Dep't of Commerce Office	(513) 684-2944
Financial Assistance	(614) 466-5420
Incorporation Information	(614) 466-1145
Minority Opportunities	(614) 466-5700
OSHA	(614) 644-2631
Postal Business Center	(614) 469-4336
Publications	(614) 466-2535
SBA District Office	(614) 469-6860
SBDC	(614) 466-2711

OKLAHOMA

Website Address	www.state.ok.us
Business Development	(405) 815-5167
Chamber of Commerce	(405) 235-3669
Dep't of Commerce Office	(405) 231-5302
Financial Assistance	(405) 842-1145
Incorporation Information	(405) 521-3048
Minority Opportunities	(405) 815-5227
OSHA	(405) 528-1500
Postal Business Center	(405) 720-2675
Publications	(405) 815-5167
SBA District Office	(405) 231-5521
SBDC	(405) 924-0277

OREGON

Website Address	www.state.or.us
Business Development	(503) 986-0123
Dep't of Commerce Office	(503) 326-3001
Financial Assistance	(503) 986-0160
Incorporation Information	(503) 378-4166
Minority Opportunities	(503) 378-5651
OSHA	(503) 378-3272
Postal Business Center	(503) 294-2306
Publications	(503) 956-2222
SBA District Office	(503) 326-2682
SBDC	(503) 726-2250

PENNSYLVANIA

Website Address	www.state.pa.us
Business Development	(800) 280-3801
Chamber of Commerce	(717) 255-3252
Dep't of Commerce Office	(215) 597-6101
Financial Assistance	(717) 783-5046
Incorporation Information	(717) 787-1978
OSHA	(800) 382-1241
Postal Business Center	(717) 257-2108
Procurement Assistance	(717) 783-8950
Publications	(800) 280-3801
SBA District Office	(412) 644-2780
SBDC	(215) 898-1219

PUERTO RICO

Website Address	www.puertorico.com
Business Development	(787) 721-2898
Chamber of Commerce	(787) 721-3290
Dep't of Commerce Office	(787) 766-5555
OSHA	(787) 787-1560
SBA District Office	(787) 766-5572
SBDC	(809) 834-3590

RHODE ISLAND

Website Address	www.state.ri.us
Business Development	(401) 277-2601
Chamber of Commerce	(401) 521-5000
Dep't of Commerce Office	(401) 528-5104
Financial Assistance	(401) 277-2601
Incorporation Information	(401) 277-3040
Minority Opportunities	(401) 277-6246
OSHA	(401) 457-1800
Postal Business Center	(401) 276-5038
Procurement Assistance	(401) 277-2601
Publications	(401) 277-2601
SBA District Office	(401) 528-4561
SBDC	(401) 232-6111

SOUTH CAROLINA

Website Address	www.state.sc.us
Business Development	(803) 737-0400
Chamber of Commerce	(803) 799-4601
Dep't of Commerce Office	(803) 765-5345
Financial Assistance	(803) 252-8806
Incorporation Information	(803) 734-2158
Minority Opportunities	(803) 734-0657
OSHA	(803) 734-9606
Postal Business Center	(803) 926-6200
Publications	(803) 737-0400
SBA District Office	(803) 765-5376
SBDC	(803) 777-4907

SOUTH DAKOTA

Website Address	www.state.sd.us
Business Development	(605) 773-5032
Dep't of Commerce Office	(402) 221-3664
Financial Assistance	(605) 773-5032
Incorporation Information	(605) 773-4845
OSHA	(605) 688-4101
Postal Business Center	(605) 357-5050
Publications	(605) 677-5287
SBA District Office	(605) 330-4231
SBDC	(605) 677-5498

TENNESSEE

Website Address	www.state.tn.us
Business Development	(615) 741-2626
Dep't of Commerce Office	(615) 545-4637
Incorporation Information	(615) 741-0529
Minority Opportunities	(615) 255-0432
OSHA	(615) 781-5423
Postal Business Center	(615) 885-9399
Procurement Assistance	(615) 741-4294
SBA District Office	(615) 736-5881
SBDC	(615) 678-2500

TEXAS

Website Address	www.state.tx.us
Business Development	(512) 936-0223
Chamber of Commerce	(512) 472-1594
Dep't of Commerce Office	(512) 936-0442
Financial Assistance	(512) 936-0282
Incorporation Information	(512) 463-5586
Minority Opportunities	(512) 936-0296
OSHA	(512) 440-3834
Postal Business Center	(512) 342-1264
SBA District Office	(512) 888-3333
SBDC	(214) 860-5831

UTAH

Website Address	www.state.ut.us
Business Development	(801) 957-3480
Chamber of Commerce	(801) 467-0844
Dep't of Commerce Office	(801) 524-5116
Financial Assistance	(801) 269-8408
Incorporation Information	(801) 530-6027
Minority Opportunities	(801) 538-8829
OSHA	(801) 530-6901
Postal Business Center	(801) 974-2503
Procurement Assistance	(801) 538-8790
Publications	(801) 538-8775
SBA District Office	(801) 524-3209
SBDC	(801) 255-5991

VERMONT

Website Address	www.state.vt.us
Business Development	(802) 728-9101
Chamber of Commerce	(802) 223-3443
Dep't of Commerce Office	(617) 424-5990
Financial Assistance	(802) 828-5627
Incorporation Information	(802) 828-2371
Minority Opportunities	(802) 828-5237
OSHA	(802) 828-2765
Postal Business Center	(800) 230-2370
Publications	(802) 828-3080
Procurement Assisance	(802) 828-5237
SBA District Office	(802) 828-4422
SBDC	(802) 728-9101

VIRGINIA

Website Address	www.state.va.us
Business Development	(804) 371-8253
Chamber of Commerce	(804) 644-1607
Dep't of Commerce Office	(804) 771-2246
Financial Assistance	(804) 371-8254
Incorporation Information	(804) 786-3733
OSHA	(804) 786-6613
Minority Opportunities	(804) 786-5560
Postal Business Center	(804) 775-6224
Publications	(804) 786-5560
SBA District Office	(804) 771-2400
SBDC	(804) 371-8253

WASHINGTON

Website Address	www.state.wa.us
Business Development	(360) 753-4900
Dep't of Commerce Office	(206) 553-5615
Financial Assistance	(360) 753-4900
Incorporation Information	(206) 753-2896
OSHA	(360) 553-7520
Postal Business Center	(509) 626-6733
Publications	(360) 664-9501
SBA District Office	(360) 553-7310
SBDC	(509) 335-1576

WEST VIRGINIA

Website Address	www.state.wv.us
Business Development	(304) 558-2234
Chamber of Commerce	(304) 342-1115
Dep't of Commerce Office	(304) 342-1115
Financial Assistance	(304) 558-3650
Incorporation Information	(304) 345-4000
OSHA	(304) 558-7890
Postal Business Center	(304) 340-4248
Publications	(304) 558-2960
SBA District Office	(304) 347-5220
SBDC	(304) 558-2960

WISCONSIN

Website Address	www.state.wi.us
Business Development	(608) 266-9884
Dep't of Commerce Office	(414) 297-3473
Financial Assistance	(608) 258-8830
Incorporation Information	(608) 266-3590
Minority Opportunities	(608) 267-9550
OSHA	(414) 521-5188
Postal Business Center	(608) 246-1245
Procurement Assistance	(608) 266-2605
SBA District Office	(608) 264-5261
SBDC	(608) 263-7794

WYOMING

Website Address	www.state.wy.us
Business Development	(307) 777-7284
Dep't of Commerce Office	(303) 844-6622
Financial Assistance	(307) 777-7284
Incorporation Information	(307) 777-7311
Minority Opportunities	(307) 777-4457
Rural Development	(307) 777-6581
SBA District Office	(307) 261-6500
SBDC	(307) 766-3505

APPENDIX VIII
DOING BUSINESS WITH
THE U.S. GOVERNMENT

This appendix provides information on making the United States Government a customer for your product or service.

The United States Government is the world's largest purchaser of goods and services to the tune of over $225 BILLION dollars annually. Virtually everything you can think of is purchased in both large and small quantities. So, have no doubt that whatever service or product your business is selling it is being sought by this prolific buyer! Also, get the idea out of your head that the Government only deals in large purchases. Sure, they buy airplanes and submarines for billions of dollars but in fact this level of buying accounts for less than 5% of all Government purchases. The majority of purchases are for $5,000 or less.

Furthermore, and equally important, the U.S. Small Business Administration (SBA) has a mandate to make sure small businesses obtain a certain percentage of everything the government buys. Because of this, nearly all government agencies have special small business programs that are designed to ensure this mandate is met. The SBA also operates electronic bulletin boards as well as a page on the Internet. Don't overlook them as a source of information and assistance.

Now then, how can you possibly pass up a customer like this? So what's the catch? None, really. There is a perception that doing business with Uncle Sam is so hard that the trouble is not worth it. The secret to selling to the government is to be knowledgeable about the process. Here are a dozen initial steps you can take that will put you on the road to making the largest customer in the world yours!

1. Determine the Standard Industrial Code (SIC) code for your products or services. This code is used by many agencies when purchasing and you will need it when filling out various forms. SIC codes are listed in "The Standard Industrial Classification Manual" (700 pages!) which is available at most larger libraries. Check the reference section. You can also purchase your own copy from the Government Printing Office for $29. Call them at (202) 512 1800.

2. Get a CAGE code. This is an alpha-numeric identifier assigned by the Defense Logistics Services Center and identifies your business. CAGE numbers are used by many government purchasing activities to identify the firms with which they do business. This code is especially important if you want to sell to any of the Defense Agencies. You obtain a CAGE code by first contacting the agency with whom you are interested in doing business or an authorized Procurement Technical Assistance Center (PTAC) who will complete a portion of Form "DD 2051." You then complete the form and submit it to:

> Defense Logistics Services Center
> ATTN: DLSC-FBA; Federal Center
> 74 North Washington
> Battle Creek, MI 49017-3084

There are too many PTAC's to list but here a couple. Contact one nearest you and ask for the contact information of the PTAC that serves your area:

Economic Development Council of
Snohomish County
Contact: Teena Kennedy
Manager / Procurement Technical
Assistance Program
917 - 134th Street, Southwest, Suite 103
Everett, WA 98204
Phone: (206) 743-4567
Fax: (206) 745-5563

University of Nebraska at Omaha (NBDC)
Board of Regents
Contact: Gerald D. Dalton
1313 Farnam-On-The-Mall
Omaha, NE 68182-0248
Phone: (402) 595-2381
Fax: (402) 595-2385

Long Island Development Corp
Contact: Sol Soskin
Director, PTAC
255 Executive Drive
Plainview, Long Island, NY 11803
Phone: (516) 349-7800
Fax: (516) 349-7881

3. **Ensure that each agency with whom you might do business has a copy of your SF-129** (Solicitation Mailing List Form) so that you will receive copies of any solicitation from that agency. Copies of this form may be obtained from virtually any government agency. Simply call and ask for the "Small Business Representative." Review the U.S. Government section of your local telephone

directory for numbers. You can also get copies from the General Services Administration Business Service Center in your area. Call 202 708 5804 for the office nearest you.

Also check with the SBA who can assist you with determining which agencies may be interested in your product of service. Call them at 1 800 827 5722.

4. **Visit or call** the office of any government agency in your area and talk with the small business representative about selling to their agency.

5. **Get listed in PASS**. This is the Procurement Automated Source System which provides a central referral system of small businesses interested in selling to the government. This can bring you business with almost no effort at all and it's free! Get a PASS application form by calling the PASS hotline at 1 (800) 231 7277.

If you are a minority owned business, get listed in ABELS (Automated Business Enterprise Locator System), another important database. Get an application by calling the Minority Business Development Agency at (202) 482 1958.

6. **Review the Commerce Business Daily** (CBD) for contract awards to determine sub-contracting opportunities and to check which agencies are purchasing your product or services. You may find copies of the CBD at most large libraries, you may subscribe at a cost of $260/year by contacting the Government Printing Office at (202) 512 1800, or best of all you may view the current issue for free on the Internet at: http://cbdnet.access.gpo.gov

7. **Share ideas with local companies** doing business with Federal government agencies. Most newspapers carry listings of companies that have won government contracts.

8. **Market directly to other contractors, state and local agencies** who receive Federal contracts. Find who they are by reviewing the CBD.

9. **Pursue micro & small purchases**. Most agencies purchase millions of dollars of products in amounts of $5,000 or less. Make sure that you indicate you are interested in these small purchases when you talk with the various agencies.

10. **Ensure that your company brochure is in the hands of every procurement agency you can locate**. Try to get it into the hands of the small business representative for each agency that purchases your product or service. The small business representative can be located by calling various agencies (local numbers if a facility is near you) or their Washington, DC headquarters. Simply ask. Additionally, your local SBA office may have lists of contacts.

11. **Visit or call your local SBA office** and ask for assistance and ideas. This will be time well spent!

12. **Obtain a merchant card account** (accept credit cards for payment). Most agencies are now using credit cards for purchases less than $2,500.

GENERAL INDEX

D

E

L

M

N

O

P

payroll taxes...*See* taxes
personal guarantee 124
personal liability 29, 30, 34, 48, 122, 127
planning.. xiv, 63–77, 105

R

risk 7, 13, 15, 58, 81, 126, 166, 209

S

saving money.. 204
SCORE 204
SF-129 Form...xviii, xix
SIC code 291
Small Business Administration (SBA) 290
sole proprietorship ....xviii, 54
    advantages.. 27–30
    disadvantages... 27
speaking... 197
strategic plan
    goals.. 66, 69
    mission... 65, 67
    progress reporting 66, 72
    risks.. 15, 22, 66, 70, 71, 74, 88, 133
    scope 22, 66, 68, 74, 139, 146, 156, 175
    strategies 66, 71, 105, 108, 175, 200, 235
    vision 65, 66, 67

T

tax forms
    Form 1040.. 39, 41
    Form 1065.. 29, 39, 41
    Form 1096... 29, 39, 41
    Form 1098.. 42
    Form 1099.. 37, 39, 42, 164
    Form 1120.. 39, 42
    Form 941... 39
    Schedule SE 39, 41
    SS-4 42
    SS-8 .... 147, 151
taxes
    Federal tax deposit coupons.. 42

U

W

Z